WHEN RUNNING IS NOT ENOUGH...

Become More Than You Ever Thought Possible

The author's own story of how he became a runner, marathoner, Ironman triathlete, and author who's books have inspired people from all over the world to become more than they ever thought possible.

By

Ray Faut

CW00551493

Author of

Ironstruck... The Ironman Triathlon Journey

Ironstruck Revised, Updated Second Edition

Ironstruck? 500 Ironman Triathlon Questions and Answers

Lifestruck...A better way for today's youth

Triathlete In Transition-Common sense guide for new triathletes

Seniors On The Move

It's Kona Calling

The Nomad Club...Never wander alone again

WHEN RUNNING IS NOT ENOUGH

Become More Than You Ever Thought Possible

CONTENTS

INTRODUCTION

Writing a book about my life was something I had never given much thought to. I always felt it unlikely that people would find it all that interesting.

However over the past few years my thinking on the subject has changed.

So often when I do a book signing session people ask questions about my past career as a runner and a triathlete. I have such a passion for the Ironman, running, and fitness in general, that I seem to just start talking and before I realize it, ten minutes have gone by and I seem to have the full attention of my audience.

At first I was always found myself apologizing for talking so much, but pretty well everyone seemed to find what I had to say intriguing or interesting in one way or another so I finally stopped apologizing.

I also found it really surprising how many people I come across who seemed to feel that life was leaving them behind and it was too late for them to make positive changes. They were too old, or too out of shape, not athletic enough, were over-weight, or simply didn't believe they could do it.

So much of this sounded a lot like myself about three decades ago. I felt that if wrote this book and perhaps inspired at least a few people with my story, then it would be well worth the effort.

I'm convinced that many people are their own worst enemies when it comes to improving the direction their life is going. A person may be unhappy and often dream wistfully of doing great things, but might lack the self-confidence or perhaps the self-esteem to move forward and take their life in a new, more rewarding direction.

In their mind *others* always seem to be better looking, have more confidence and are more intelligent. *Others* have the best jobs, the best family, and the best home, and for the wistful athlete *others* are seemingly stronger, jump higher, run faster, and can run further.

So many of us are conditioned to believe that the laurel wreath of victory and success is reserved for the select few who breathe the rarified air at the front of the pack.

I suppose that might be true if victory in life were only measured by beating everyone else at whatever we are attempting to accomplish, but victory or *winning* in life can come in many different forms.

To my way of thinking, being a winner can be summed up in very simple terms regardless of the athletic event, game, contest, relationship, career, or any other life situation that comes your way.

When the dust settles and the results are in, do you feel better about yourself than you did before the proverbial gun went off? Do you feel uplifted, proud, at peace with yourself, and happy to be alive?

I didn't mention anything about coming in first because for most people in the world, being first is not necessarily a prerequisite in order to have positive feelings about how they performed and what they gained from an experience.

Who are we to judge what is or isn't a victory when it pertains to someone else? What we assume is a failure or perhaps a resounding success might not be how the doer of the deed envisions the outcome.

Take for instance a 10k road race where the eventual first place finisher is disappointed with the result because he was 10 seconds to slow for the $500 bonus he set out to win for breaking the course record. In his mind, he failed even though others think he is a winner because he came in first.

At the same time a 45-year-old woman walks and jogs slowly, doing the best she can and finally reaches the finish line long after the awards have been handed out and most of the other people have gone home.

Ray Fauteux

She is dead last yet is in tears and rejoicing because in the past two years she has lost 70 pounds and has just accomplished something she thought she could never, ever do.

She may well have just changed her life for the better forever, and the result of the day is a resounding victory for her and would most certainly feel uplifted and proud.

To me, these seem like feelings that a true winner in life would experience and would be well worth any effort and sacrifice it might take to get there.

I have come to believe that success inspires even more success and once we take on *any* seemingly impossible challenge and succeed, it opens up the door to a whole new world of possibilities. Sure, there is always the risk of failure, but we may never realize our full potential if we don't at least try.

The alternative is to simply give up and do nothing and be a spectator in life and as the years pass relentlessly by wonder what might have been.

This is exactly where I found myself almost 45 years ago, and is one of the reasons that prompted me to write this book for you.

I know exactly what it's like to be unhappy with the direction life happens to be going. But I also know that making positive change is possible if one is willing to take a leap of faith and perhaps a bit of a risk. There is always a chance of failure, but there will *never* be success without at least trying.

In my travels over recent years I have also met many successful runners who claim they would love to run a marathon but don't know if they can do it, or marathoner runners who would love to take on the Ironman challenge but can't swim and feel it's something they could never learn.

Whatever your background, I'm sure you will enjoy reading how I went from a loser in life to a runner, marathoner, triathlete, Ironman, and an author who has inspired many people around the world to change their lives for the better.

What you might find especially interesting is that every one of these accomplishments seemed insurmountable to me when I first considered taking on the challenge they represented.

So if you need a bit of inspiration to get your life moving or perhaps to simply take it in a different direction, you might really enjoy reading my story. Or if things are going just fine for you, but you just enjoy reading, I sincerely hope you find "When Running's Not Enough" an enjoyable and interesting book.

It's a good thing, because under the circumstances it most likely would have been a natural progression for losers like us.

Pretty well all the idiot things we did were compulsive in nature. What had seemed like fun back then as a teenager was really a pattern developing that would impact the way my adult life would unfold.

It's an unfortunate reality that far too many people who are born into a dysfunctional family environment will often have to deal with the consequences of their shitty luck for the rest of their lives in one way or another.

Of course not everything we did was fueled by drinking and much of what we did was just teens being teens and we did many of the same things teenagers around the world do today.

The Summers in Vancouver seemed to go on forever back then and we spent glorious days at the beach and our favorite spot was English Bay. We would spend hours memorizing the latest hit songs word for word. In those days it was the Beach Boys who were topping the charts and then this weird English group called the Beatles came along, but there was this one song in particular that we memorized and I have never forgotten and it best describes the hot, lazy Summer days of the Vancouver I grew up in.

"Hot town, Summer in the city,

Back of my neck's getting dirty and gritty.

Been down isn't it a pity,

Doesn't seem to be a shadow in the city.

All around people looking half dead,

Walking on a sidewalk hotter than a match head.

Even though it's some forty years later I still hear that song from time to time on an oldie but goodie radio station and the memories come flooding back like it was yesterday.

2

You might wonder why I have no hesitation when it comes to sharing my thoughts about my less than stellar youth, but I truly believe it's better to face the ups and downs of our lives head-on as opposed to pretending they never happened. Keeping things bottled up doesn't seem like the healthiest alternative.

It really doesn't matter who we are, success is all the sweeter and inspiration to others more powerful if we don't hide the darker side of our lives and shortcomings that ruled us before we were blessed with success and good fortune.

To not have humility and hide our failures is not a true picture of ourselves, because in reality everyone has a cross to bear at one time or another in the course of their lives and none of us is perfect.

It's finding ways to overcome obstacles that life throws in our path that really count the most. It's how we make the most of the untapped wealth of gifts that lay dormant within all of us that is the truest measure of who we really are.

I feel no shame at all in sharing with the world that I ended up being a smoking, drinking, partying fool for a good decade after leaving high school. I simply adopted the compulsive behavior that had become the norm for me through the crucial formative years of my youth.

The only difference was that instead of Vancouver, I lived in Toronto before finally settling in Calgary for most of my adult life. But really, it makes no difference where you live, you can't run away from who you are.

There's no doubt in my mind that the way we are when we leave the school years behind is not going to change that much when that door closes behind us and we head out into the *real* world.

There is no definitive line in the sand and the transition from a teenager into adulthood is a seamless one. As far as social skills, self-esteem, and self-confidence go, what you see is pretty much what you get.

I partied, drank beer, and smoked through most of high school because I believed that if it was good enough for my dad, then it was good enough for me. When we are young and impressionable, our dads are our heroes and could do no wrong in our eyes. By the time some of us realize that all dad's *are not* heroes it's often too late and the emotional and physiological damage is done.

It only seemed natural to carry on with the same social behaviors and bad habits into my twenties because really, that was the only way of life I knew.

When marriage came along you might think that it would bring about a change in these ingrained habits, but actually I went from a single fool with bad habits to a married fool with bad habits. It just so happened I came across a woman who was anxious to marry an idiot....I guess.

I had little regard for the state of my heath and could have cared less about fitness. At 28 years old my weekends consisted of drinking a few dozen beer, smoking maybe 50-60 cigarettes, and simply doing nothing.

There was no doubt that my life was on a downward spiral and unless some drastic changes were made I was at risk for all sorts of problems on many different levels.

At the very least my quality of living in general and overall life expectancy would be on the low side of the longevity scale.

I think deep down I knew that something had to change but I didn't know what to do or how to begin. It was not lost on me that there should be more to life and I was somehow squandering my time in this world.

I truly believe that I continued on the way I was for so long because nothing ever came along that motivated me to take my life in another direction. There was never a goal or a reason strong enough to convince me to change the way I lived my life and I needed a miracle.

I needed something to wake me up and get me out of the deepening rut I found myself in. As the years have passed I have come to the realization that each of us has a wealth of possibilities within us just waiting for some sort of catalyst to bring them to life.

I believe many people live their entire lives without realizing their full potential. It's so easy to fall into the sameness and routine of our everyday lives while the years are flying by and opportunities are slipping away.

Some of us are just lucky enough to have that one spectacular moment in our lives when we witness, hear, or read something that galvanizes us into action and sets our life on that new and better course that changes us for the better, forever.

For me that moment happened one day in the Summer of 1976.

RUN FOR YOUR LIFE

For me it was just another Saturday afternoon much like dozens of Saturdays that had come before it. There I was laying on the couch smoking a cigarette and channel surfing. My trusty bottle of Old Vienna beer was close at hand. Actually, it was in my hand.

It was Saturday July 31, 1976 and call it what you like, but by a stroke of fate, destiny, or divine intervention I happened to be channel surfing and landed on the late stages of the Olympic Marathon in Montreal.

An East German by the name of Waldemar Cierpinski was just entering the Olympic Stadium to the cheers of some 50,000 spectators. He was all alone as he circled the track and headed toward the finish line.

For some reason it was a moment that captivated me.

I was transfixed by the drama unfolding on the Olympic track. In hindsight I believe it was because I lacked any personal goals or aspirations to make more of my life and I was witnessing this at a time when I was vulnerable and desperately in need of inspiration. Besides, I had become very good at being a spectator, and like many people still do, often lived out my dreams through the accomplishments and success of others.

Here was this runner all alone in front of a packed stadium within sight of the finish line. I was so impressed that he had run over 26 miles and was only seconds from the finish line.

Of course I had heard of marathons, but always considered them a feat only a very few people were capable of. I never in my wildest flights of fantasy ever thought it was something that I could ever attempt.

How could I possibly? I was in such poor physical shape and basically unhealthy from the lifestyle I had chosen to live since my early high school years.

Except that day something different was happening.

I had this sense that something very special was taking place, but didn't know what. I felt this sudden urge to take some sort of action. At that very moment in time, I sensed an awakening of something deep inside me that I never knew existed.

It was ultimately that singular moment that eventually brought me here, almost 45 years later writing and sharing this story with you.

I remember watching the marathoner's that day and thinking "I wish I could do something like that". Then it was "maybe I can do something like that". Then unbelievably, "I'm going to do that!"

That afternoon in July as I watched runner after runner reach the finish line of the Olympic Marathon I made the decision that day I was going to start running and I was going to run a marathon of my own.

2

Five months would pass and during that time I never let go of that moment of inspiration and the idea that was firmly planted in my mind on that Summer afternoon simply would not go away.

Well, we've all heard about New Year's resolutions. Most have us have committed to one or several of these at one time or another in our lives.

In January the fitness centers across North America are always inundated with new members and the diet books are flying off the shelf at record pace.

Running shoe sales sky-rocket and spiffy spandex disappears from fitness clothes racks as the newly resolute plan their New Year aerobics, yoga, or kick-boxing campaign that is meant to whip them into shape.

Final clouds of putrid cigarette smoke are sucked into already blackened lungs on the last day of December and half full packages of cigarettes are flying into garbage containers at an unprecedented rate.

Yet despite the best intentions and resolve of so many, most resolutions quickly begin to lose steam. Soon, most people are right back into the bad habits that inspired them to make a change for the better in the first place. They have come to the realization that it takes work and can be very challenging to change the course of one's life for the better.

The spandex finds its way to the fitness gear graveyard in the far corner of the closet to join cousins from failed resolutions of years gone by.

Diet books become garage sale fodder or paper-weights, and purses, dresser drawers, and inside suit pockets are searched frantically for a long lost package of cigarettes that is calling out loud and clear.

Over the Christmas holidays of 1976 I made a resolution to become a runner and chase my marathon dream. As the new year unfolded I began my quest to adopt a healthier, more vibrant way of life.

It was a resolution that would not die and almost 45 years later it is still my guiding light and the decision I made so long ago to simply "become more" has remained with me to this day.

3

I really didn't have any running gear. I rummaged around in the closet until I found the ten dollar pair of running shoes that I wore when I cut the lawn. They were covered with grass stains and one of the shoe-laces had broken and was tied together with a knot.

The only shorts I had were dress shorts. Back in those days, the big fad was to wear dressy matching t-shirts and wool shorts. The t-shirt usually had a breast pocket for your cigarettes. Those days they were especially cool because they had front and back pockets perfect for carrying my wallet, spare change, car keys, address book, comb, cigarette lighter, and beer bottle opener. Not in a million years were they meant to be running shorts but I really didn't have a clue what I was doing.

I figured that wearing the matching top was probably pushing the envelope of running decorum and settled on a plain white t-shirt.

So there I was standing in front of the mirror all dressed up and ready for my foray into running. Baggy blue shorts, white t-shirt, and grass-stained runners. I was born to run......not.

It's one thing to have a resolution, but it's another thing altogether to put that plan into action and take those first few small steps of your journey along the road of self-discovery and toward a better way of life.

I had no idea where to start. I was completely lost.

I knew there was no way I was going to just go outside and start running in front of God, the world, and the nosy neighbor down the street. I had zero self-confidence and could not have possibly been more self-conscious as a result.

Also, there were other factors to consider.

You have to remember that in the 1970's you would never see dozens and dozens of people running all over the place no matter what city in the world you happened to live in. People were more into being spectators and it was only a small percentage of the population who seemed to be into competitive sports or fitness in general.

The birth of the true fitness and running boom was a decade away and seeing someone run along the river path was an oddity and not a regular occurrence in Calgary, the city where I was living at the time.

There were stories of runners being stopped by the cops and asked what they were running from and of people stopping their cars and calling out to a runner, "Is everything okay! Do you need any help! Do you need a ride!"

I remember the day when one of the veteran Calgary Roadrunners said to me, "sometimes I think I should run with a hubcap under my arm just for the Hell of it just to see what happens."

In many ways I felt like I was venturing into a world where I really didn't belong. I couldn't possibly have been further from being a runner. I had no knowledge about running and years of smoking and drinking had made me so unfit, that the notion I had of becoming a runner seemed like a foolish idea.

Who did I think I was that I could even consider doing anything like this?

Yes, I was full of doubt, but in those early days I hung on to that one shining moment of Olympic inspiration that had given me a brief glimpse of what might be possible.

Now at last I had a goal–a dream–and something very special to aspire to and I was not about to let it go. I hung on to that dream for dear life until I found the perfect place to begin my running career.

I finally happened onto the YMCA in the North end of the city and discovered they had a gymnasium where I could begin to run in

Ray Fauteux

relative obscurity. For a small monthly membership fee I could run around the perimeter of the basketball court to my hearts content. There was no track to run on, but for me the gym was perfect because I could go late in the evening when there were not many people around.

When I walked into that gym on the evening of January 3, 1977 to hopefully begin my journey to the marathon finish line, I really didn't know what to expect or how to even begin.

I should clarify something here and at the same time leave a suggestion for you that you might want to consider.

I decided in the very beginning that it would be more motivating for me if I recorded everything that happened. This was especially true in the early years of my running career. My feeling was that if I could continue to see progress on paper, it would inspire me to keep going.

I have scrapbooks dating back to 1977 that has pages coming loose from the spine. There are newspaper clippings that are more yellow than white, but because I have kept them, all the time lines and race information you will read in this book is accurate. So for example, if I say I began running on January 3, 1977 for the first time, that's exactly when it was.

Regardless if you are a weekend warrior, a pro athlete, or someone completely new to sports, I would really consider recording everything because decades from now you might have kids, or grand-kids who would love to look at the old pictures. I can almost guarantee that years later you will enjoy looking back on those days yourself and reliving the memories, and besides, you might decide to write a book about your own life one day.

So anyway, there I was, all decked out in my spectacular running gear and ready to go. Sure, it sounds simple enough I suppose. Just start running. Everybody knows how to do that because when you think about it, genetically the instinct to run is a natural ability that is ingrained in all of us. It was true when the cavemen were running after the elusive Mastodon and true 2500 years ago when

Pheidippides ran from the plains of Marathon to Athens in the Summer heat to proclaim victory over Persia.

But there was more to it for me. I was so out of my element. I couldn't even remember the last time I had run anywhere. Plus there were other people in the gym that first night shooting a basketball around and the last thing I needed was an audience.

When you have no confidence in yourself, it seems to magnify the difficulty of pretty much everything in your life.

It's like when you walk into a weight room for the first time ever and you are surrounded by buff, muscular, super-fit people and you feel like the equivalent of a 90-pound weakling. You have no idea how to do the exercises, use the equipment, or even how much weight to use.

You kind of cringe inside and feel like everyone is watching your every move.

I really think that this type of inferiority complex is one of the main reasons why people who make a resolution to get fit soon give up on it. They cannot get past the feeling of inadequacy and simply choose to go back to the familiar and mundane comfort of the way things were.

That's about as close as I can come to describing how I was feeling that night. So there I was looking up at chart on the wall of the gym that said 24 laps around the gym was one mile. Well, I had to start somewhere and decided my goal for that first night was to run one mile. I had no idea how far that could be under the circumstances. I had no concept of running distances and what was short and what was far.

Well, I ran about 10 steps and thought right away, "this is going to be really hard." Even before I finished the first lap I was getting dizzy and there were black spots floating in front of my eyes. This was most likely caused by years of heavy smoking and not enough oxygen getting to my brain or anywhere else where it was needed for that matter. No doubt the oxygen was probably having trouble

Ray Fauteux

navigating through my black lungs and this made any sort of physical exercise more challenging.

Or to put it another way, my entire body was saying "what the Hell is going on out there! Stop what you're doing right now!"

But it was damn the torpedoes and full speed ahead and I forced myself to do three laps of the gym. I really didn't get my money's worth that first night because after that I was pretty much done.

It was in those first moments when I stopped running and gasping for breath that I fully understood for the first time the magnitude of the abuse I had put my body through over the years and the uphill climb I had in front of me.

In the very beginning I knew the cigarettes had to go and they had to go right away.

I got in the car and sat out there in the parking lot before heading home. My very first training session lasted all of a seemingly endless five minutes.

You might think that my first instinct would be to simply give up on this foolish notion I had of running a marathon, but actually the exact opposite happened. It was while I was sitting in the car thinking about what had just happened that I made what would become one of the most important decisions of my life.

If ever I was going to give up on my far-fetched dream, this was the time when I was most vulnerable, but realized with a certain clarity that I was pretty much at ground zero as far as fitness and that I had nowhere to go but up. Something told me that all this was happening for a reason and that I had to persist.

That same night I gave up a 13 year smoking habit and made up my mind that I would give myself a chance and would keep right on trying. It was the last day I ever smoked. This decision that I made after my first foray into the world of running turned out to be monumental and would change the course of my live forever.

I believe when it comes down to making life-changing decisions like this you have to put aside the life you led up to that point and embrace a new beginning.

Perhaps Mother Teresa figured it long ago when she said:

"Yesterday is gone and tomorrow isn't here yet. We only have today."

4

In the first week the improvement in my running seemed agonizingly slow. It was a battle and I had to fight for every lap around that gym. I went back night after night and willed myself into doing just one more lap. I was sure that if I persisted it would start getting easier, and that's exactly what happened.

Even though I kept getting dizzy and continued to see spots every time I pushed too hard to finish just one more lap around the gym, my breathing became noticeably easier with each passing day.

I have to admit that it was extremely hard to just give up smoking after all those years, but it was my goal to run a marathon that helped me make through the nicotine withdrawal. To this day I believe that it's not patches, pills, hypnosis, or acupuncture that are the surest ways to give up the smoking habit. It's the desire to do something or achieve something important that smoking makes difficult or impossible. I discovered that this is the most effective way of giving up the habit.

In other words, what you are trying to accomplish provides more of a high and more of a reward than cigarettes ever will. It was all the inspiration I really needed to give up the habit.

A few years ago I saw this poster in my doctor's office. It stated that even after a week of not smoking a person's lungs would begin to clear up. In a matter of months, or weeks in some cases, the improvement in breathing and energy levels would be very noticeable.

After two years and sometimes less, lungs would clear up and be pretty much as healthy as they were before one began to smoke. I believe that by running and quitting smoking at the same time I accelerated the recovery process and the difference in the way I felt was nothing short of incredible. Because it was a habit that began back in my teens, I had no idea just how much of a negative impact it had been having on my physical health. Right or wrong, it had simply become a way of life.

It was a real milestone for me when I finished 24 non-stop laps after just two weeks. It was the first mile I had ever run and from that day on my self-confidence began to grow.

By the third week I ran 5 miles in the gym and that was the signal for me to take it outside. Running all those corners in the gym was making me crazy anyway and it seemed like the right time to take my running to another level.

At this point I was running pretty well every day and the compulsive nature that was ingrained in me since childhood became my best friend. Instead of drinking and smoking, my addiction became running and that's a trade-off I would take any day.

As my confidence grew, I didn't care what anyone thought. I was on a mission and it was such a great feeling to feel and see the improvement in myself. It seemed so much easier to reach the 10 mile barrier once I had the confidence that I could do it.

By the end of six weeks on February 16, 1977 I had recorded a total of 100 miles of running. By March 9th I was at 200 miles, March 24th 300 miles, April 9th 400 miles, and April 30th, 500 miles. As you can see, I began to run further and further in less time. Once I knew I could run for an hour, it just made sense that if I persisted I would be able to run for two hours and then three hours, and that's exactly what happened.

In what seemed like a very short time to me I found myself just days away from my May 1 date with the start line of my first marathon.

There was just one more thing to do. I was going to have to find myself a decent pair of running shoes for the big race. Someone pointed me toward a tiny running store that was being run by a former pro football player.

I really didn't know what football players had in common with running shoes, but I decided to give it a try because I didn't know where else to go.

His name was John Forzani and I walked into his shop and told him I needed a pair of running shoes for my first marathon. He disappeared into the back room and came out with the ugliest looking running shoes I'd ever seen. They were bright yellow and were called *Tigers*.

I shit you not. Tigers. They even had stripes.

Well anyway, I put those things on because I didn't have the heart to tell him that the shoes he picked for me were really ugly. Besides he was a 250 lb.+ ex-pro lineman or something and I thought it was best to stay on his good side.

Then he gave me a pearl of running shoe wisdom that I have never forgotten. "Now you don't want them so tight that your nose will bleed."

He seemed to have his heart set on unloading these shoes so I thought what the Hell, they don't feel that bad anyway, so I bought them. It was a sign of how far I had come since day one. I mean, in the beginning the last thing I wanted to do was attract attention to myself. Here I was buying yellow running shoes that did everything but blink on and off and would be pretty difficult for anyone to miss.

It seemed that my self-confidence had grown in step with my running ability and I really didn't care anymore what anyone thought. I was a runner and proud of it. Besides the yellow runners were a great match with my navy blue dress shorts that I decided to wear for the race. Okay, so they were a match from Hell, but I needed pockets for my car keys and stuff.

So sue me.

So now I was ready for the big race and my dream was close to becoming a reality. I could hardly believe that the day arrived so quickly. It seemed like I had just struggled to run my first few laps around the gym and in the blink of an eye the big day had arrived.

5

There were just over 100 runners at the start line of the Calgary Marathon in Bowness Park waiting for the starting gun.

It's worth mentioning that there were only a couple of women in the race. Before the 1970's is was a common belief that women could not run in endurance races and for the most part the marathon was a male-dominated sport.

So no matter what country where a marathon was taking place, it was these early women marathoner's who were special and very courageous. They were the forerunners of women marathoner's and endurance athletes all over the world.

It would be 1984 in Los Angeles before the first women's marathon would take place in the Olympic Games and today women make up pretty much half of any marathon race.

As I stood on the line waiting for the starting gun, I can't really put into words how exciting and exhilarating it felt just to be there. It was so special to be part of the charged atmosphere that I would soon learn was present at the beginning of every race no matter what the distance. I remember thinking that soon I would no longer be a spectator on the outside looking in, but would actually be participating and have others watching me.

When the gun sounded, I didn't really have a plan in mind and just ran with complete abandon as fast I could manage. So, I just went out with the leaders thinking that maybe I could win the race or something.

No kidding. I actually thought that.

Of course the more experienced runners began to pull away from me in the first 10 minutes and I didn't care, and just kept right on running as fast as I could. There were several loops in the race so you would see other runners who were in ahead of you in the race coming back towards you. I was getting some really strange looks

Ray Fauteux

from some of the hard-core Calgary Roadrunners. It was looks of surprise and it wasn't until after that I figured out why.

I was just so thrilled to be running and to be part of the race that I felt like I had wings on my heels and it was just so good to be where I was and to be living the dream that I had imagined.

My recorded time for the first 10k was 40 minutes. So if you do the math, I was on a pace for a marathon time of around 2:50. At the time I was running in about 7th place and that's why I was getting those looks of surprise.

Thinking back I suppose those other runners were wondering, "who the Hell is that guy?" You have to remember that the distance running community was not that big back then, and everyone pretty well knew everyone and I guess I caught them by surprise.

Anyway, you can pretty much surmise that something had to give. At the 20k mark I was at 1:22:48 and still on track for under 3 hours and at 30k I was at 2:12:20 and it was about at this point when I had my first of many encounters with the mystical "wall" that mysteriously appears on every single marathon course in the world. I hit that wall so hard that I'm almost certain that somewhere about 30 miles away there was a farmer out in his field who looked up and said "what the Hell was that!"

Of course it caught me completely by surprise but I just kept right on going. I was really hurting and running a lot slower now but there was *nothing* that was going to stop me from reaching the end of the marathon that was just over 10k away.

As I entered Bowness Park and was just a few minutes from the finish line, I was pretty much overwhelmed with what was happening and what I was about to accomplish.

The official time for my first ever marathon when I crossed over the finish line was 3:28:49. I ended up in 34th place of the 100 starters and none of that really mattered. What did matter was that with just four months of running I had gone from the couch and a life going nowhere to the finish line of a marathon. I had in essence begun a journey that has still not ended some 45 years later.

It would be many, many years and dozens of marathons later before I would realize that under the circumstances just how amazing the results of that day truly were on so many levels. At the time it never really dawned on me because I was just so happy to be able to run and be part of something that had seemed so out of reach and so impossible for me to even contemplate.

There was no way for me to judge what was a good or bad result, because I had nothing to compare those early results with.

That first marathon began a whirlwind of races as I embraced running and the thrill of road racing with a passion.

Less than five weeks later I ran in the Canadian Marathon Championships in Edmonton. I discovered early on that one of the best things about being a runner is that you can be in the same race with some of the best no matter what your own ability level is.

The race was actually a test of what was to be the upcoming Edmonton Commonwealth Games marathon course. Jack Foster from New Zealand, an Olympian and medal winner was there by invitation and of course won the race.

There were some pretty weird things that transpired that day for me as I took on my second marathon. First of all, my race number for my first marathon and was 12, and my number for my second in Edmonton was 13.

My finish time in Calgary was 3:28:49 and my official finish time in Edmonton less than 5 weeks later was 3:28:59. I'm not even sure what this means, but it was very strange to me that my first two marathon times were just 10 seconds apart. This is especially weird when you consider all that can happen over 26.2 miles of running.

One of the main purposes for writing this book is to inspire people and perhaps if possible, pass on a few lessons along the way that I learned from years of trial and error.

I really want you to look at the results and the time splits from these two races closely.

CALGARY MARATHON SPLITS:

10k............40:00

20k............1:22:48

30k............2:12:20

Finish........3:28:49

Those numbers each represent a section of the race. I was about a quarter of the way through the race in 40 minutes. Just short of the half-way point of the 42k marathon, I was still under the 1 hour 30 minute mark. By the time I had reached 30k I was beginning to run out of energy and slowed down big time after hitting the wall and the last 12k of the race I was just barely able to hang on.

EDMONTON MARATHON SPLITS:

10k...........44:45

20k...........130:07

30k...........2:17:08

Finish.......3:28:59

Although I finished my first two marathons in almost exactly the same time there is a huge difference in the way I arrived at the finish line.

If you look at the two races and the time it took me to finish each section, it's obvious to me that the running Gods were trying to teach me something but I never picked up on it. As a matter of fact, it would be a few decades before I would truly begin to understand that "pace" is the secret to success for pretty much any endurance event.

I really didn't do it by design, but I ran slower in the second marathon because I was tired. After my first marathon I just kept right on running and "rest" was not a concept I really understood. So I believe I ran slower because that's all the energy I had on that day.

The concept that sometimes you have to run slower to race faster eluded me even though it was right there in front of me. It took almost 5 minutes longer to reach the 10k mark in my second marathon. All my splits were a lot slower but there is one in particular that is important to grasp.

I reached the 30k mark almost 9 minutes slower in the second race, yet my finish time is identical within 10 seconds. So what that tells me is that I never hit the invisible wall nearly as hard and maintained a better pace in the late stages of the race.

In theory, if you do the math, I could actually take "50 minutes" to reach the 10k mark and be right on pace for a 3:30 marathon. So if you are planning your first marathon or have run many and keep hitting the wall with the force of a Mack truck you might consider balancing your race-pace.

Take your projected marathon time and divide it into 4-10k splits. Add on about 10 minutes or so for the last 2k depending on your overall pace. So for example, if you feel that a 3:30 marathon is within your capabilities and you set this as your goal then don't do what I did and run the first 10k in 40 minutes. You might want to try around 48 minutes.

If you are hoping to run a 3:30 marathon, why would you go out at speed that is on pace for a 2:50 marathon, a time that is far beyond your ability on the day? You might do it because like me, you have a legitimate excuse and don't know any better. Unfortunately it's almost always a recipe for disaster and ends up being a long and very painful struggle to the finish line.

The end result will never change if you keep doing an endurance race the same way time after time. Usually it happens to the same people over and over because nobody ever takes the time to explain

Ray Fauteux

it to them and race after race ends up the same. Well, now someone has explained it to you and if you buy into the concept of pace at least you can create a structured plan instead of simply running until there's no gas left in the tank.

"Insanity is doing the same thing over and over again and expecting a different result." Ten Step Program words to live by.

6

After that second marathon, I was pretty much hooked on running and it sort of took on a life of it's own.

I entered as many races as I could and at first I didn't really care what the distances were. My next two races were 10-miler's and I went in 63:42 and 62:45 and it became a distance that I would seldom run. Ten mile races and half marathons were distances I could never get used to.

I think it was because I found it difficult to judge the proper pace. You can't really run as fast in a 10-mile race as you might in a 10k race without hitting the wall and you can't run as fast in a marathon as you might in a half marathon.

I sort of looked at the 10-mile and half-marathon as odd distances and over time the 10k and marathon would become my favorite distances to run.

It would be November 13, 1977 before I would run my very first 10k race. It was called the Herald Road Race and was very popular at the time. It started in downtown Calgary and it was my first experience in a race with a lot of runners. There were 500+ entries in the race. Back in those days that was considered a pretty big race as far as local races went.

I really fed off the charged atmosphere of these races and with this field there was plenty of adrenaline flowing. For some reason the 10k race distance was very highly contested and this particular race drew some really good runners. It also drew people like myself who were running rookies.

I was becoming a totally different person by now. My entire attitude had changed and I had become very confident in my ability and no longer felt self-conscious. I was so confident in fact that I worked my way right up to the front with all the high-end, speedy runners before the gun went off.

Ray Fauteux

Once again I had no race plan because I had never run one of these, but my thinking was that if I could run a marathon than I should be able to run like a bat out of Hell at this distance. So much like my first marathon I went in blindly and decided to run as fast as I could and stay with the leaders for as long as possible.

It was really brash considering I was still new to running and was still about 4 months away from reaching the one year mark of my running career.

It was simply remarkable when the gun went off. Did those guys ever take off! I stayed with them as long as I could. When I got to the mile mark the time that was shouted out was 4:54. Holy Crap!

I could see the leader and the other faster runners spread out over about a block ahead of me. There was no way I was going to sustain this pace. The leader must have gone through that one mile mark in around 4:40. It would be the only time in my career that I would run a sub-5 minute mile in a race. I was on pace for around a 32 minute 10k and there was no way that was happening.

The bastard's must have brought over that same wall from the marathon and plunked it down on at about the 7k mark of the 10k course because I ran right into it again.

However with such a short race I was able to keep it together and at least keep on running. By the last mile I was probably down to about a seven minute per mile pace but at least I didn't stop.

My official finishing time was 35:33 and it would end up being the second fastest 10k I would ever run. I simply was not capable of going under 35 minutes no matter how hard I tried over the years.

My official time left me in 20th place overall of the 528 starters. The winner went in 32:15. So considering I had him in sight at the mile mark you can see how far over my head I was. But still it was pretty thrilling to be able to run up there with those guys even if it was just for a mile.

The winners name was Louis Groarke and he was one of a set of triplets. They all had these long pony tails, weighed about 110, and could run like the wind. Louis was also a Rhodes Scholar.

So big deal. I finished grade 12.

Well, just about.

I ran in the original Forzani's Mother's Day 10k race the following May and there were around 300 entrants. Yes, the race was put on by the same football playing running shoe guru who sold me the yellow Tiger running shoes. Actually, they turned out to be pretty good shoes.

In years to come this race would have over 10,000 entrants and has become a fixture on the Calgary running scene.

My second 10k was pretty much like my first one and I finished in an official time of 35:21. This would be as fast as I would ever run a 10k race.

I always seemed to be able to finish in the top 5% of the field of any road race and to me having fun running meant going out as fast as I possibly could and beating as many people as I could to the finish line. I only seemed to have one speed in the 10k and it was all out. It would be years before I figured out how to pace this distance properly so I didn't feel like death for the last two miles.

I was blessed to actually be able to win a race and be first overall. It was a smaller race out of the city and there were about 70 entries. I had come in second in two different races where the 32-34 minute runners didn't show up. So that left it open to the next tier of runners who could go 35-36 minutes for the 10k.

I say blessed because is was quite an experience that I would only have once and it was something that always seemed to be reserved for the gifted few. So it meant a lot to me to at least live that moment one time and see what it was like at the front of the pack.

It's a really incredible feeling and I can see why people will spend their entire lives trying to be the best at something when it comes to

Ray Fauteux

sports. The oxygen is a lot thinner at the front and it's take no prisoners all the way. No matter what the race, you're going up against the best that day has to offer if you plan on running at the front.

I took off with the leaders as usual and this time I could sense other runners running in my draft trying to stay with me. It really surprised me when one by one they started dropping off the pace. Finally it was just two of us running together with 2 miles left to go. I was thinking that I would never be able to stay with him when he said, "I can't do it, good race," and he slowed down.

Wow! Was I surprised. I realized I was going to win and with a mile left I looked back and I could hardly see him.

7

Consider this an interlude in my story so I can pass on to you what I learned over the years about running in a 10k race.

As I said before, this book might be my story, but it's also about sharing what I learned over the years that might help out others in their own quest for fitness or better race results.

Like most of my early years of running I did pretty much everything wrong. I wasn't lacking in enthusiasm or effort, but certainly was lacking in knowledge about endurance running that can take years to figure out.

I seemed to reach a peak as far as finishing times early on in my career, and then as the years passed by my 10k times became slower by 30 seconds and then a minute, until finally I was unable to break the 36 minute barrier anymore.

It was almost 12 years later when I was in my 40's before I discovered the optimum way to run a 10k race that enabled me to break 36 minutes again and run times comparable to the times I ran when I was 28. I never surpassed my best time of 35:21, but I was able to break the 36 minute barrier again on several occasions.

When you think about it, most people who run 10k races run their first mile the fastest and their last mile the slowest because they are running out of gas and burning out at the end.

I discovered that if I reversed this way of thinking I would have less stressful races. I was 100% right, but what it also did was get me to the finish line quicker as well.

I planned my 10k races so there would be 3 acceleration points. I also planned to run my last mile faster than any of the miles before it.

So in effect my first mile was one of my slowest miles. When the gun went off I would run at a fast pace, but a pace I could easily

Ray Fauteux

handle. For example I would get to the first mile mark in 5:50 or 6:00 minutes. If you remember in my first race I was at the mile mark in 4:54 and imploded when I hit the wall at about mile four in the race.

It takes discipline to run slower than you know you can run and many people will take off ahead of you, but you have to let them go and run your own race and stick to the race strategy. Keep telling yourself that you will be passing most of them later on in the race, because believe me, you will.

So say you are running at 75% or your maximum when you reach the mile mark. At that point you make your first acceleration and pick up the pace to say 80%. If you do this right and follow the plan, I can almost guarantee that nobody will pass you for the rest of the race and you will be passing tons of people.

This is true because of one simple reason. Almost everybody goes out too fast when the gun goes off and the slow down as the race progresses. So if you are accelerating as they are beginning to slow down, there is no way they can pass you back providing you maintain your pace.

You maintain that speed until the 5k mark and this is where you have your second acceleration. Now you are possibly running around 85% of your maximum. In other words you are still not running all out, but you are running faster than you were in the first mile.

Now you are passing people by the dozens. You hold this pace until the one mile to go mark and this is your final acceleration point and this is where you run at your maximum capability all the way to the finish. When I would time this mile on my watch it would be about a 5:30-5:40 mile which was around 30-40 seconds faster than my first mile.

This is probably the only point in the race where you will be feeling any fairly intense physical stress, but that is off-set by another advantage. You are passing runners in the last mile who simply cannot respond to your speed. They are probably running their slowest mile of the whole race and your are running your fastest.

It is very uplifting to be passing others as you get closer and closer to the finish line and it actually makes that last mile fun.

It doesn't really matter if you are trying to run a 60, 50, 40, or 35 minute 10k, I really believe this is a strategy worth trying. It may take a few races to fine tune it but in the end I think the results will be well worth it.

Just to give you an example, this is a story about what happened to me with another member of the Calgary Roadrunners during a 10k race when I was in my 40's.

I was using this same strategy and had just accelerated at the 5k mark when I went running past this guy.

After the race he said, "were you late for the starting gun?"

I said, "what do you mean?"

"Well you went by me so fast, I thought you were trying to make up for lost time."

It was really pretty funny because he was 100% serious. He could not figure out how I could be running so fast and yet was so far behind him from the start. He had no idea that I had gone out slow intentionally and of course he took off at the starting gun along with everyone else. I ended up beating him by a minute and a half.

Well a month later I was in another 10k race and used the identical strategy. The same guy came up to me after that race and said. "Wow! Did you ever run that last mile fast!

He said he decided he would follow me through the whole race and he said he was doing pretty well until the last mile when I really took off and he couldn't keep up. But in the process he unwittingly ran 60 seconds faster than he'd run in the past few years and was only 30 seconds behind me.

So basically he used my strategy by following me and accelerating

Ray Fauteux

whenever I did during the race. I wonder what he was thinking when that first mile was so much slower than he was used to? Chances are he thought his time was going to be really slow because of it.

It took me a lot of years to learn that strategy and I hope you try it out if you are a fan of 10k racing and want to try for your best result. The worst that will happen is that you will not suffer as much in the last half of the race because you have better control of your pace through-out the race.

And a race with less pain is never a bad thing.

8

At the end of my very first 10k race where I ran the 35:33 time one of the more experienced members of the Calgary Roadrunners who finished about one minute ahead of me that day said, "now a 3 hour marathon is a reality for you."

I had asked him a few weeks earlier what it would take for me to be able to run a three hour marathon one day.

It seems they would take a 10k time and use it to determine a possible finish time for the marathon. Assuming of course that you would run a marathon at a much slower pace. The theory was that if you could maintain around a 5:45 or so pace in a 10k race then it should be doable to maintain a 6:50-6:55 pace for the marathon which would bring you in under 3 hours.

Back in those days the Calgary Roadrunners would head West every February and run in the Seaside, Oregon marathon. It was a sea level race and the theory was that this was the race where you could run your best time possible as opposed to Calgary that is at a much higher altitude.

The downside was that we had to train long distances during the Calgary winters that saw many more -30 degree days than we do today. It was during those years that I learned how to run in extremely low temperatures and often would run up to 3 or 4 hours at a time. Most of it came down to knowing how to dress properly in layers.

On February 28, 1978 just 13 months after my first day of running I was at the start line with 1500 marathoner's from all over Canada and the United States and several other countries. God, I thought that was so many people and it *was* a lot, but now some marathons have 30,000, 40,000, and even 50,000 entries.

I was still using my *go out too fast* tactics at this point and was at the mile mark in 5:45. I still had no idea of pace and I had just run a

Ray Fauteux

mile time that would compute to a sub 2:40 marathon when all I wanted to do was break three hours. So basically I started the race running over a minute per mile too fast and once again doomed myself to a race from Hell.

It was great for about 19 miles than that bloody wall was there again so as usual I just smashed into it. The big difference between this marathon and my first one was that I was able to hold a better struggling pace up to the finish and my official time was 256:32.

I would not go under 3 hours again for over 13 years.

By my 13th month in the sport of running I had gone under 36 minutes in the 10k and under 3 hours in the marathon. It would be a long time before I would see those times again and it took years to figure out why.

It would take that long to figure out the race strategy that I just talked about. The strategy of running your first mile slow and accelerating incrementaly at predetermined points in the race.

9

It was just before my first marathon in Calgary when I reached a total of 500 miles of running since the day I first put on those grass-stained running shoes. It was the end of April, 1977, four months after I began running when I reached that plateau.

By August 5th I had put in 1000 miles of training. At the end of my first year I had a total of 2,540 miles of training recorded.

In January, 2008 at the beginning of my second year of running, I ran 404 miles in training for that month in preparation for the Seaside Marathon I just told you about. I ran another 200 miles in the first two weeks of February before we left for the race. It's safe to assume I most likely went into that race over-trained and tired, but who knew?

Running became my life and in many ways took it over. In one of the earlier years of my running career I ran 364 days. I missed a day because I was still married at the time and my wife talked me into not running on Christmas Day. Against my better judgment I took my first and only day off for that year. I should clarify that I had rest days during the course of that year, but to me a rest day was an easy 3-5 mile run. So I guess you would call it *active rest*.

I had no concept of how important *total rest* was in the equation. In fact I really believed that if I took days off I would begin to lose all that I had gained. Of course that's not true, but when you don't know any better, you live by what you believe and that's why I ran every day.

It wasn't to prove anything. I really believed I was the right thing to do in order to compete at my best. Even before a marathon I would run easy for 3-5 miles in the days before the race.

As I got to know the more experienced marathoner's in the city, they explained about taking rest days and also about tapering going into a race. So I would run for 10 or 15 days straight and then take a total rest day. I still didn't have it right, but at least it was better than running every single day.

It's probably safe to say that as the years passed, I was going into pretty much every race over-trained and tired. This probably explains why my times never improved much when I was doing all that training. My body was probably rebelling and I just didn't realize it.

Most likely the reason I ran my fastest races so early in my career was because I had not beat myself up quite as much in training as it was just my first year.

I really believe I was my own worst enemy and was stifling my own improvement because of my inexperience and lack of understanding about things like rest, diet, and tapering when it came to endurance events.

Later on in this book you will understand exactly what I mean and what a difference a little knowledge can make.

10

One day I heard about this 50-mile race that was taking place about a 5-hour drive from the city. As soon as I heard about it I was in. It was scheduled to start on a Saturday night at midnight. The organizer's did this in order to have a minimum of traffic problems to deal with.

I wasn't able to get the day off from work, but I did arrange to start at 5am so I could possibly get away early and make it to the race on time. I left right from work and I knew it was going to be a challenge to make it on time. Of course the R.C.M.P. just had to pick that night to pull me over and give me a speeding ticket.

It wasn't so much the fine I was worried about. It was the time it took for them to write the damn ticket that really pissed me off.

I rolled into town at 11:35pm, just 25 minutes before the race was due to start. I missed the pre-race meeting, but they had a girl there who would act as my support and would stay close in her car and provide water etc., or I suppose drive me back to town if I threw in the towel. Every runner had their own personal assigned "pit crew" and she was mine.

It was July 12, 1980 at midnight when the gun sounded and 14 of us headed out of town to begin our 50 mile journey.

It seemed almost surreal running out on those dirt country roads in the small hours of the morning with the only light coming from the moon, stars, and headlights of the support vehicles that quickly spread out as some runners decided to go out faster than others.

I kept the leaders in sight for as long as I could and then just settled into a steady pace as they pulled away into the night and I concentrated on just finishing the race. It was made especially difficult because it had rained the day before and the mud caked on our running shoes. It had a way of making feet feel ten pounds heavier.

Ray Fauteux

When we reached mile 27 I was in new territory and it was as far as I had ever run. By mile 35 I began to slow and it was a struggle to keep moving, but there was a force driving me that would not let me quit.

It was a pretty unique experience to be running in total darkness and then watch as dawn came and for the first time actually be able to see the country-side that surrounded us. By mile 45 I had to run and walk, run and walk for a few miles until I could pull myself together for the final push into town.

With three miles to go I ran the rest of the way into town and it was pretty special feeling to reach the finish line and finally be able to stop running completely.

It was 8:23 Sunday morning and that was my finish time for the race. I was 8th out of 14 starters and 13 of the 14 who started managed to complete the 50 mile course.

The winner was Al Howie who ran the race in 6:34:15. It must have been quite the finish because the second place time was 6:36:51 and it was discovered later that these two runners ran in excess of 50 miles because a pylon was put in the wrong spot as they reached town.

It was a pretty impressive performance when you do the math. They ran the equivalent of back to back 3:25 marathons or faster depending how much further than 50 miles they actually ran.

I have met some pretty remarkable people over my career and Al Howie was certainly one of them. He was quite the character.

Of course there was an awards ceremony and breakfast and when it was time to head home I asked Al how he was getting home because he didn't appear to have a car.

"I'm thinking of running," he said.

"So where do you live?"

"Vancouver."

"What?"

"Vancouver."

"So how far is that?"

"About 660 miles."

I knew that, but I just wanted to hear him actually say it.

The thing about this conversation is that he was serious. It turns out that he was one of the premier ultra-distance runners in the country and he was quite capable of running the 650 miles to Vancouver over the next two weeks or so even though he had just won a 50 mile race in around 6 and a half hours.

"Actually, he said, "there is something I have to do in Calgary and besides my wife will be upset with me again if I don't show up at home on time. Even at home she hates it when I go for a run because sometimes I'm not back for 2 or 3 days."

I couldn't believe I was having this conversation so I said the only thing I could think of.

"Al. Get in the car. I'm taking you to Calgary."

"All right" he said. I can take the Greyhound from there."

So that's how I ended up driving Al to Calgary. He was great company and had some pretty cool running stories to tell. By the time I got back home it was seven pm and 39 hours had passed since I crawled out of bed at 3:30am two days earlier so I could be at work by five in order to make it to the race on time.

It seemed like a lifetime ago and in that time I had worked an eight hour shift, drove for 6 hours, ran a 50 mile race and drove another 6 hours. It was almost midnight Sunday and 44 hours had passed before I could finally relax enough to fall asleep.

Such was the power of whatever it was that was driving me to run, and very soon the demands I was placing on my body were about to catch up with me.

I continued to push myself in training and ran in one more marathon before my knee finally gave out.

I had heard there was a specialist in town who was trying a new surgery technique so I phoned and was talking to his nurse about an appointment. I thought because Dr. Bell was as prominent as he was that it would be months before I would get to see him let alone have the necessary surgery.

It was a Friday morning when I called the office and the nurse said to me, "can you come in Monday morning and bring in your running shoes?"

I couldn't believe it because I thought I would lose a year of training and racing before all this was worked out. On Monday Dr. Bell looked at my shoes and my knee and said "how is next Thursday for you for surgery?"

Wow!

It turns out that he was one of the pioneers of arthroscopic surgery in Canada. To the best of my knowledge up until that point the first athlete he had performed the procedure on was a pro football player. I guess he wanted to try this surgery on other athletes and that was how I managed to get in so fast to have the surgery.

I believe I was one of the first marathoner's in the country to have the surgery that has now become common-place and has been a blessing to many amateur and professional athletes.

Normally knee surgery involved a crescent shaped incision that meant opening the knee right up. The knee had to be in a cast and the muscles would lose mass and it took months before athletes fully recovered from surgery and were able to get back into action.

I went into day surgery and was knocked out for about 30 minutes.

When I woke up the surgery was done and there were just two band-aids on either side of my knee. He had used the small incisions to put the scope in and find the problem. The cartilage(meniscus) that was causing the problem was trimmed and the surgery was over.

I was able to run slowly a few days later and exactly 8 weeks after surgery ran the Calgary Marathon in 3:15. It was really quite amazing.

Even so, it never had to happen. You would think it would have been a wake up call, but I kept right on pushing until the other knee gave out a year later had the same surgery all over again.

I just couldn't seem to get enough from running. I was always looking for more. I don't know for sure if I was running towards something or away from something, but I was certainly driven by some unseen force to keep forging ahead.

There was no challenge that seemed to be enough and I couldn't seem to run far enough to satisfy whatever need it was that I was trying to fill.

As much as I loved running and all it had done for me, I had run as far and as fast as I possibly could and felt myself yearning for something more. It was as if I was making up for lost years and was embracing the new found confidence that had basically turned me into a different person.

I had changed so much in fact that I had become far different from the uninspired partying fool my wife had married and my compulsive nature and my desire to seek out new challenges was pretty well the death knell for our marriage.

It was really nobody's fault. I think we all have to find our way in this life the best way we can, and the alternative for me would have been to live an unhappy, unfulfilled life. I really believe that if a person is unhappy, that everyone close to that person will eventually be unhappy as well.

Ray Fauteux

So there I was, single and feeling that there must be another challenge on the horizon. I had no idea what that might be, but one day in 1982 I found out.

IRONSTRUCK

In the early 1980's North America was beginning to experience a fitness boom. Actually, I should say it was more of a "running boom" than anything else.

So here I was looking for something more after basically running myself into the ground for six years when so many people were just starting to get excited about running for the first time. I had changed a lot over those six years and had stopped being a spectator in life and didn't spend hours and hours watching others perform on television so I could live my dreams through their accomplishments.

Although I continued to enjoy watching television sports on occasion, especially the Olympic Games, I was no longer in awe of pro athletes, Olympians, or anyone else for that matter. I knew now that it was possible to get out there and experience my own successes and reach my own finish lines.

Some people simply have more opportunity in life than others and that makes all the difference. For instance, what if my early years as a kid had taken a different turn? What if I wasn't side-tracked by my home environment and other forces out of my control? What if I had spent my high school years on the track team becoming a better runner?

When you consider that I began to run for the first time at 28 years old from basically ground zero, who knows what would've happened? Running a 35 minute 10k and a sub 3-hour marathon in my first year indicated that I had some natural speed and endurance. But for a twist of fate, maybe I could have been an Olympic athlete myself.

That's why I began to look at so called "super-athletes" in a different light. I began to realize there must be many people out in the world who due to life circumstances have sequestered talent and ability. I believe the reason so many of us pull for the under-dog is because we see ourselves in them and really want them to succeed.

It makes us feel better to see someone realize their full potential.

I came to understand through my own circumstances that what people really need is something or someone to inspire them to begin believing in *themselves* and by taking a leap of faith, it could be them accomplishing great things they always felt were beyond their grasp.

The rewards of gaining self-confidence and believing in oneself will far transcend sports and can touch every aspect of a person's life once it's realized that most of our limitations are ones we fabricate ourselves. Life can get pretty exciting once a person realizes they are just as capable of being in the limelight as they are of being a spectator.

It's one thing to watch the same people cross the finish line first over and over again, but it's another thing completely to watch someone give all they have just to reach that line at all. To me those are the people who are the true heroes and winners in life.

That's the very reason why there was one sports television show in particular that I watched whenever possible. It was called ABC Wide World of Sports. I thought it was a very special show because they didn't just show winners and their motto "the thrill of victory and the agony of defeat" pretty much said it all.

It showed athletes had great success but also those who didn't. Amateur or pro, the show was about people who were trying their best regardless of the outcome and I think that's what made the show special.

That and the fact that some of the failures were spectacular in nature.

It was a Saturday in the Fall of 1982 when I tuned into my favorite show already in progress. I saw all these spectators cheering as runners were crossing this finish line and thought I was watching a marathon somewhere. Then I began to realize that this was much more. Yes, they were just finishing a marathon all right, but I was shocked to learn that they had also done a 2.4 miles swim in the ocean and bike 112 miles *before* the marathon.

I couldn't believe it.

I had never heard of a triathlon at all until that very moment. I thought it was quite an accomplishment just to run a marathon–and it was–but how the Hell could these people swim that far and than bike that far and *then* run a marathon.

Holy crap!

I was mesmerized as this woman named Julie Moss came staggering down the last 50 feet towards the finish line. She fell and got up and fell again and only had a few more feet to go to cross the line. Up until than she was the first place woman but there was another woman closing in on the finish and she was getting closer and closer.

I'm thinking, "why doesn't she just get up and cross the line? Get up! Get up! Get the Hell up!

But the other girl passed Julie before she was able to get back up and cross the finish line. If ever there was an ultimate agony of defeat moment in the world of sport, I had just witnessed it. However, it was also the thrill of victory as she never quit even when her body did. After she was passed and lost first place she never quit. It took her thirty seconds to crawl the last 50 feet to the finish line.

Of course at the time I had no idea what Julie Moss and all the others I was watching had gone through just to get to the finish line. I knew nothing about this event called the Ironman Triathlon that was going on in Kona, a small fishing village on the big island of Hawaii.

I began to learn a lot more about it as they showed people struggling to reach the finish line long into the night. It was surreal to see them cross the line under the glare of the ABC camera lights.

Ray Fauteux

What was especially compelling was the fact that it was obvious that it was a victory for every one of them and they were all winners in their own right. I thought, *these people are nuts. I have to go there. I have to cross that finish line.*

Once again I was inspired by something I witnessed and just like the first time it had happened six years earlier, it would change the course of my life once again.

Although I was afraid of the water and could not swim a stroke to save my life, I felt that I could overcome the fear and somehow learn how to swim. If I could get off the couch and realize my dream of running a marathon, than I could find a way to do this.

I was so completely swept up by what I had seen that I felt myself being drawn toward the Ironman like a moth to a flame. I really didn't know what was compelling me to go to Kona. I just knew that I was going to do whatever it took to get there, of that I was certain. One day I would cross that finish line under the camera lights in Kona.

2

There was one major stumbling block in my way. There was no getting around the fact that I had to get into the pool and somehow learn how to swim.

It was Winter of 1983 when I returned to the YMCA and the very place I had first learned how to run. It seemed like an eternity ago and now and I had gone full circle and arrived back where it had all started.

It was a whole different challenge I was facing this time when I found myself in the pool for my very first swimming lesson. I wasn't refining my stroke, or learning how to swim smoother or faster. My main concern was how I was going to survive in water over my head without going under.

I will never forget the first words my swimming instructor said to me. "If you want to do this Ironman thing, you'll have to let go of the side of the pool."

So that's where I began. They gave me kid's lessons for adults. They taught me how to hold my nose and bob up and down in the water. They taught me how to take my very first real swimming stroke. Then one night I swam from one wall to the other in the open water with nothing to hang on to for the very first time in my life.

It was a width, not a length. It would be a few more lessons before I was ready to go the entire length of that 25 meter pool.

Once I had the confidence and ability to make it to the far end of the pool I knew it would just be a matter of persevering and eventually I would be able to go further and further. Because I had become a successful endurance runner I had the belief in myself that I could accomplish just about anything if I persisted.

I swam day after day. I was driven to get it done. I never let that finish line in Kona get far from my thoughts and that was what inspired me to keep on going. I had a very inefficient energy-wasting stroke but I didn't care. I just kept on swimming further and further as the weeks passed.

Then one day I swam my first mile. It seemed to take forever, but it was a huge victory for me. I kept on plugging away and six months from the time I took my very first lesson, I swam two miles in the pool non-stop.

I felt that if I could swim two miles in the pool than I could somehow find a way to swim the entire 2.4 mile swim leg on race-day and that was good enough for me.

Ironman Hawaii 1983 had come and gone when I sent my entry in for the 1984 Hawaii Ironman in Kona.

In the early 80's there were no qualifying standards necessary to get into the Ironman. At that time there was a category for foreign contestants and because I was Canadian I was able to enter.

The number of Americans allowed into the Ironman was already being limited in order to make it more of an international event. The Americans had begun to realize before the rest of the world that this extraordinary event called the Ironman Triathlon was something special.

The Ironman was starting to attract more and more attention on a world level. How could it not when the three main sponsors for Ironman Hawaii at the time were ABC, Timex, and Bud Light?

About a month after mailing in my entry form I received a letter from Kona.

"Congratulations, you are now entered in Hawaii Ironman 1984."

I have to admit, it was both scary and exciting. Once again I was heading into foreign territory and soon would be taking on what was at the time, the most challenging endurance event in the world.

3

Over the course of 1983 I met other novice triathletes in Calgary who were intent on taking on the Ironman challenge. They were quite a diverse and very special group of people.

Even though we came from different backgrounds and had different goals in life we all had one thing in common. We had all become *Ironstruck* and although we didn't know it at the time, the unseen force that was calling us to Kona and this event called Ironman would be just as powerful decades later.

Eventually there were ten of us and we decided to form a team and go to Hawaii together for the Ironman. We needed a name so I came up with "Try-Ten" because we were going to Kona to "try" and finish this thing.

There were three women and 7 guys. One of the women had aspirations of being in the Iditarod dogsled race one day. Another girl, Julia was into an event called "ride and tie" that involved running beside your horse, and on your horse, and orienteering at the same time. I'd never heard of it up until then but it sounded pretty interesting.

We had a banker, a few guys who were married, and a guy named Chip who owned a surf clothing store in downtown Calgary. Yes it was Calgary and yes, it was a surfing store. There was also Grant who had aspirations of being a fitness coach one day.

It was helpful to be around these people because I was able to learn a lot from them. Most of them could swim pretty well but there were three of us who struggled with it and were basically in foreign territory when it came to swimming in general, but especially swimming in the open water.

I had no idea what to get as far as a bike was concerned so they pointed me toward a bike shop called, you guessed it, The Bike Shop. I would get to know Kevan the owner really well and at the

Ray Fauteux

time he knew about as much about triathlon as I did, which was pretty well nothing.

He sold me this $400 Norco bike. Someone put a decal on it that said "triathlon" so that made it a triathlon bike I guess.

I would go out on training rides with some of the other Try-Ten team and they would leave me in the dust as most of them had riding experience.

I had no idea how to train, how far to ride, or even how to ride a road- bike properly and I found it every bit as challenging as swimming. I would go out on the highway until I thought I had gone what seemed like a pretty long way and then turn around and go back home. A long way out to me was 20 or 25 kilometers so with the return trip 40 or 50 kilometers was about as far as I would bike in my training.

I never truly understood what I was getting myself into and my few 50 kilometer rides were a bit short of the 180 kilometer bike leg of the Ironman. I didn't really care. I was going anyway and that's all that really mattered.

I decided early on that I would just do what I could and let the chips fall where they may.

So one early morning in the Fall of 1984 myself and most of the rest of the try-ten team boarded our Wardair flight to Kona, Hawaii. There seemed to be two schools of thought when it came to acclimatizing to the heat and humidity of Hawaii. Either go a few weeks before the race to get used to the environment or go a day or two before the race so your body wouldn't know what hit it.

Most of us opted for being there two weeks beforehand and were on the same flight. I booked 3 weeks for Hawaii so I would be there for a week after the race. I mean why not? It was Hawaii and I was single.

The flight out of Calgary was great. There were only about 50 people in total on the Wardair 747 on a direct flight to Oahu. When we arrived we boarded our connecting light on Aloha Airlines to Kona on the Big Island and it was about this time that I was getting pretty apprehensive about what I was getting myself into.

For almost two years the Hawaii Ironman had seemed to be a distant and at times unattainable dream, but reality hit when we touched down and rolled to a stop at the airport in Keahole, about seven miles from Kona.

Ray Fauteux

4

Arriving in Kona was surreal. The air was charged with a mixture of excitement and anticipation. Part of the excitement for us was the relief that usually comes at the end of a long flight. The warm tropical breeze drifting in from the ocean was quite a departure from the cold winds that had just begun to gust in from the North as we left home.

There were bike boxes everywhere, much like the one Kevan at the Bike Shop had helped me pack my bike in. Bike bags or bike cases made specifically for traveling by air were still a few years away from becoming readily available.

That afternoon there were people arriving from all over the world and what made it so remarkable was that no matter what country people were from, we had all somehow managed to feel the same irresistible pull of the Ironman and all had a common goal.

Little did we know at the time that this same invisible force would one day be the clarion call for tens of thousands of ordinary people from every corner of the world. Ordinary people who would become extraordinary by taking on the challenge of the Ironman.

As I stood there at the Kona airport taking in the electric atmosphere I looked at the people all around me. There was a group of Japanese athletes just arriving. Except for the United States, Japan would have the most entries in Ironman Hawaii 1984 with around 100 Ironman hopefuls making the trip from Japan. If you listened carefully you could hear Australian, British, and German accents in the din of voices emanating from the arrivals area of the airport.

There was this one girl I will never forget. I tell this story every chance I get because something about her struck me as being very special. I don't think her 5'3" body weighed much more than 105 pounds. She had straw-colored hair that was cut into a short "bob" cut and her piercing gaze and the resolute way she held herself told you there was much more to her than met the eye.

She had an old, well-used bike, but the spokes sparkled and the gear cluster gleamed in the tropical sun and you could just tell she had spent hours caring for that bike so it would get her to where she was going. She had a khaki-colored, army-type backpack slung over one shoulder, and had on a t-shirt that said *If you're looking for trouble you can stop. It just arrived.*

Gotta love her.

So there she was in all her tiny, powerful glory to take on the most difficult and challenging endurance event the world had ever seen up to that point in time. It was hard to believe that just a decade earlier it was felt that women lacked the stamina and endurance to run a marathon.

"Can anyone share a cab to Kona!" I heard her call out as our taxi pulled away for the trip to town. I don't think she would have had any trouble getting a ride. It wouldn't have surprised me in the least if she didn't even have a place to stay and was planning to sleep on the beach.

I often wonder about her and how her Ironman turned out. You just know she would have found her way to the finish line. She may have had just a beat up bike and a backpack for luggage, but it was her indomitable spirit and courage just for being there that I had no doubt would have seen her through to the finish.

It was a remarkable time and Kona was a place full of remarkable people.

5

One of the guys in the group had found us a place to stay that was pretty much ideal and we had booked our rooms a month before we arrived. The Sea Village had big, spacious rooms with fully-equipped kitchens, a barbecue area, a pool, and most of all a great view over Kailua Bay and the Ironman swim course.

Well, actually maybe the part about over-looking the swim course wasn't all that great for me. For at least a little while almost every day I would sit on the sea-wall and look out over that course and at the marker that was set at the 1.2 mile turn-around. I couldn't believe how far away it looked from the shore.

I had never had an actual swim in the open water and a mile in the pool back home somehow didn't seem nearly as far as a mile in the ocean appeared to be. I'm sure the more experienced swimmers among us were not nearly as concerned, but for someone who couldn't swim one width of the pool one year earlier it was pretty unnerving. I suppose the biggest difference was going to be not having the security of the end of the pool to hang on to if I got into any sort of trouble.

It was going to be swim or sink from the looks of things.

The Sea Village was right on Ali'i drive and was actually situated on part of the bike and run course. It was about a five minute bike ride from the Sea Village down to the center of town and the start/finish line. The first thing I did was bike into town to the super-market to do some shopping. It was when I returned and went out to the pool that I first realized how many other triathletes were staying at the Sea Village.

It was so easy to meet people and talk to them because pretty much all of us had something in common. It seemed that everyone in Kona was either a local, was entered in the Ironman, or knew someone who was.

There was an American guy and his girlfriend staying at the Sea Village who were really interesting. They cruised around on his yacht for most of the year and he had done most of his bike training and running on an exercise bike and treadmill on the deck of the yacht. Of course swimming was no problem because they lived on the water. She told me, "he's the captain and I'm the cook." Some cook. She was a striking blonde with stunning blue eyes who could cause car accidents just by walking down the sidewalk.

Then there was the sisters from Winnipeg. They weren't in the race, but were there to cheer on their brother. It would take another book to write about the sisters. They loved their beer and they loved to party and because I was single they spent most of their spare time in my room.

There were so many single woman around that every time I opened a closet door I stood back in case a woman fell out. Didn't they know I had to conserve my energy? Damn.

There were far worse places to be than in Hawaii in 1984 if you were a single guy and a triathlete. But I was on a mission and bit the bullet and behaved myself. When I think back it was pretty funny because I was just so focused on the Ironman that anything to do with woman just went right over my head.

Well, at least until after the race.

Most afternoons everyone would be laying around the pool sun-tanning, reading, or listening to a Walkman.(yes, I did say Walkman) CD players and I-pods were still decades away.

We would all be immersed in thought, lazily enjoying the warmth of the sun and the breeze whispering in from the ocean and Chip the beach whale would do a belly-flop in the pool and soak everybody within a kilometer of the pool.

Chip was around 250 pounds and would be the biggest person in Ironman Hawaii 1984. He was quite a character and one day he said, "Ray, c'mon for a cappuccino"! It was then that he told that he could live in Hawaii for about $10 a day if he had to.

Ray Fauteux

I guess he had actually done it and was a surfer dude at one time and was no stranger to sleeping on the beach in Hawaii. I believe it because when you're as big as Chip was you can probably sleep wherever the Hell you want. His story also explained the surf shop back home in Calgary.

Julia was one of the girls on the team and one day I was in Julia's room visiting(she was waiting for her fiance to fly in)and we were sitting there shooting the breeze and Chip walked in and Julia offered him some Cornflakes.

Chip said "sure" and went to the cupboard and got a salad serving bowl that I'm sure would have held enough salad for eight people and he filled it almost to the top with cereal. He just kept shaking and shaking the crap out of that Cornflakes box until it was just about empty. Then he poured about half a quart of milk in it and sat down and began shoveling it in. I was impressed because he didn't use sugar.

Julie sat there with her mouth open and looked at me and we broke out laughing and Chip just kept right on shoveling until he finished the whole bowl.

You just never knew what Chip was going to do next. He was such a free spirit and it was great to have him on our try-ten team. He sort of had this quality that made people not take things quite so seriously and take time to relax. Believe me, it helped in the days leading up to the Ironman.

Years later when Chip created his Lululemon empire and went on to become one of the five richest people in Canada it really came as no surprise.

The keys to his success were probably a combination of the way he had with people and his unique way of thinking.

Good for him.

6

In the two weeks leading up to the race, it would be safe to say that we did pretty well everything wrong as far as preparation. To begin with we were going in with a decided disadvantage compared to the triathletes of today.

Of course there were no training books, coaches, diets, triathlon clothing or equipment available to us that would help us get through the Ironman.

Lets face it, the bike I had with me for that Ironman was a piece of metal with wheels. There were no aero-bars, swift-shifters, snap-in pedals, bike computers, titanium, or anything else for that matter that would make things easier on race day. By today's standards our bikes were incredibly heavy and not having aero-bars would ultimately make the bike leg of the race exceedingly more difficult. Of course that in turn would impact the marathon.

I didn't really have anything to wear for the swim other than a swim suit, and wanted something I could wear on the bike as well. I saw a note on the bulletin board down by the beach about something called "tri-shorts" some guy from the States was selling from his room. I had never heard of them but went to check it out.

They were perfect. They came down to about mid-thigh and were perfect for the swim and were padded for the bike so that's what I would wear on race day for the first two legs of the race. I bought a t-shirt from one of the expo tents that matched the red pair of running shorts I had brought along and I would wear those for the run.

I had another stroke of good fortune when I found someone selling swim goggles called "Barracuda's". They were amazing because back home I had spent two years trying to find a pair of swim goggles that fit me properly and didn't leak. Usually I would have to wear them so tight that I would get a headache, but the Barracuda's had a soft foam padding and sealed perfectly without

Ray Fauteux

being overly tight.

Everything about the Ironman was so new that even the equipment was being invented on the fly. Nobody had really started creating gear strictly for triathletes because the event was in it's infancy and there wasn't much of a market at the time.

When it came to rest or tapering, most of us had no idea what to do. So we did what you would expect and kept right on training. Personally, I picked up right where I left off in my running career, training too much and resting too little.

We would get on our bikes and ride for miles out on the Queen K. Highway in the heat of the day. We would go on ten or twelve mile runs. Some people were swimming the course every other day. I sure wasn't. I would go out a little ways and come back.

Once I was past 50 meters, that was as far as I had ever swam without the edge of a pool to hang on to. When I tried to swim further it was a disaster and I'm almost certain there those among the group that were worried that I would not be able to do the swim on race day.

Gord, who had done several smaller triathlons was one of the better swimmers and one day he got to swim the whole course with the Puntos Twins from Montreal. At the time they were two of the top women triathletes in the world.

Just the same, pretty well all of us were doing way to much when we would have been better off laying around the pool or in the shade. Every bit of energy we used up was pretty much unrecoverable in time for race day.

We had a minor disaster when two of the guys, Tony and Pierre, heard about this 100 mile bike race that was taking place a week before the Ironman and decided to do it.

Unbelievable. But that's just the way it was.

Tony became so dehydrated that he ended up in the hospital and would be unable to compete in the Ironman. It would devastate him for a long time and I can fully understand it.

There was also a lot of posturing in the days leading up to the Ironman. We were proud that we were there to take on this challenge and wanted people to see us running, swimming, and out on our bikes. We felt special because in many ways, we were.

When you consider that less than a decade earlier the marathon was the marquee endurance race in the world. Now this thing called Ironman had come along that threw in a 2.4 mile open water swim and 112 mile bike ride *before* the marathon.

It's no different today. People who have what it takes to accept the Ironman challenge are just as special and feel the same way we did.

Years later, when I was at Ironman Canada doing book signing's I still see novice Ironman Triathletes doing exactly what we did in 1984. And you know what? Although it will do them no good on race day and might actually have a big negative impact on their race, I say go ahead and do it.

You will only ever have one first Ironman and you should enjoy every bit of it. Just know that burning up energy you will never recover in time for the race may greatly impact your race day results. As long as you are aware of that and willing to risk it, I would say go for it and enjoy the moment.

If that means running ten miles and then swimming the entire course than do it. If it means a 75 mile bike ride in the heat of the day four days before the race, than do it. Get out there and let people see you. You have earned the right to have your moment in the sun.

It's the completely wrong thing to do from a rest standpoint, but you have to do what feels good to you and as you continue on with your career you will eventually figure out for yourself that it's wise to temper your enthusiasm.

Ray Fauteux

7

It was the day before the race and we were relaxing around the pool when Chip came up with another gem that would forever be at the forefront of my first Ironman memories.

"Okay guys" he said. "I booked a beauty salon for us. We're all getting shaved for the swim". As usual none of us knew what the Hell he was talking about, but soon he explained it to us.

It turns out that Chip used to be a competitive swimmer and when he competed he always shaved all the hair off his arms, chest, and legs and it made sliding through the water easier and according to him made him faster.

Right.

Well, if nothing else it was a much needed diversion considering we were all pretty much on pins and needles about the next morning so most of us guys went with him to get shaved.

The hair salon was closed for the day and there they were, these three gorgeous Hawaiian women with electric shavers in their hands and glints in their eyes waiting for us to show up.

It was really hilarious and we took some great pictures as they ran those shavers up and down our legs and arms and across our chests. Thank God we would be wearing swim caps because if Chip had his way, I think there was a good chance we would have left there bald.

"Now" he said. "You have to go back to your room and take a razor and shave again until you are completely smooth. You have to get off that fine layer of hair that the shaver didn't take off."

Who was I to argue. I mean the damage was already done, so there I was back in my room breaking out the package of disposable razors when there was a knock at the door and the evil sisters from Winnipeg were standing there. I told them to could come in, but I had to shave and I told them what was going on.

"Oh! We'll help" they said.

Oh for God's sake. What next?

So there I was standing in the bathtub with these two hot chicks in the tub with me shaving my arms and legs and chest. They were having a good time so who was I to ruin the party? And yes, I was wearing running shorts.

The whole body shaving episode started by Chip was actually the perfect diversion and after the sisters left much of the day was gone and all that was left to do was get things ready for the morning.

I spent an extra long time looking out over Kona Harbor from the Sea Village as the day was winding down. You could see the boats full of volunteers stringing out the buoy markers for the swim course.

They had these huge inflated bright orange markers spaced out every few hundred meters from the swim start at the wharf to the Captain Bean glass bottom boat that was anchored at the turn. Once we swam past the Bean boat there would be a sharp right hand turn, a short swim of a few hundred yards and than another right hand turn for the 1.2 mile return trip to the finish of the swim leg and to our bikes that would be waiting for us in the transition area on the wharf. As I looked out over Kialua Bay I think it was the first time in my life I felt apprehensive, afraid, excited, and happy all at the same time.

With all the doubts creeping in the day before the race, I kept telling myself that it was a pretty big deal just making it this far. It was in that very first year that I began to understand that just getting to the start line of the Ironman was a huge accomplishment. There were just so many things that had to come together and so many obstacles to overcome in order to make it possible.

Over the years that would never change for the Ironman triathletes of the world. They would all have to overcome their our own set of road blocks in order to make it to the swim start of an Ironman and at least have a chance at reaching the finish line.

Learning how to swim or bike, finding the time to train, juggling the hours in a day to fit in work, and family as well as training all take their mental, physical, and emotional toll. Then there is the expense of equipment, traveling, accommodation, entry fees, and a myriad of other costs to deal with along the way.

Then after all the training and all the sacrifice, an injury can stop your dream in it's tracks. So yes, as I sat there thinking about the day ahead, I knew I was fortunate just to be in Kona and to at least be able to give it my best shot.

It was a restless night of sleep and as I drifted off I could almost hear the whispered challenge of the Iron Gods carried by the ocean breeze that drifted in through the open window.

We're waiting, we're waiting to see what you're made of.

IRONMAN HAWAII, 1984

It was race morning and it was still dark when we began the walk down Ali'i Drive to the swim start area.

I was wearing my newly purchased *tri* shorts and I remember these girls walking behind us and one saying to the other "nice shorts" so I knew I had truly arrived and made the leap from my first marathon navy blue wool dress shorts to my *state of the art* (at least in my own mind) triathlon shorts.

So the morning started out on a positive note anyway, but soon I was going to learn why you always have to be ready for the unexpected when it comes to the Ironman.

As the time left before the swim start began to quickly dwindle the anticipation in the air was palpable. It was not lost on me that soon I would be facing demons of doubt and fear as I ventured into what was for me the unknown challenge of a long open water swim. Not just any swim, but a tumultuous swim in the midst of hundreds of others who were facing this challenge called *Ironman* for the first time.

It was in this lull before the storm that there was a last chance to get the tires pumped up on my bike. We had been warned that it was not a great idea to pump the bike tires up to full pressure when leaving them in the transition area over-night. The logic was that the high humidity might increase the pressure in the tires and they could possibly burst.

At the time I didn't know if it was true or not, but when you have no idea what you're doing and have no experience to fall back on it seems only natural to believe just about anything you hear. You're afraid not to just in case the advice turns out to be right.

So there I was pumping up my front tire about 15 minutes before the swim start of the biggest race of my life when there was this loud "bang!" It was totally unexpected and was like a gunshot and everyone looked to see what was going on. There was an audible gasp from those who heard the tire blow.

When I think back on it, it was really playing with fire to only bring along one spare tire. At the time it seemed only logical to me that the odds of having two flat tires out on the bike course were pretty slim. Of course I didn't take into account that I would need that spare before I even got on the bike.

I took that single spare tube and struggled to get it into the tire as the start of the race got closer and closer. I finally managed to get the tube in and began to pump it up. I was horrified to see the tube begin to bulge out of the tire like a black balloon.

I had bought new tubes just for the race and had put them in the tires the day before checking my bike into the transition area. I only put a small amount of air in them at the time so I had no way of knowing what would happen when I pumped them right up to the 100 psi that I was told was about right for the race. It seems that I had bought the wrong size tubes.

I was frantic because in those days you were on your own. If your bike broke down you were out of the race. So if I blew one more tube, my Ironman would be over before it even started.

I thought. "This is not how it was meant to be. I'm here for a reason and this can't be how it ends".

So I did the only thing I could think of and opened the valve and begin to let air out until the tube went back into the tire. That's where I left it and when I pressed down on the tire it was soft and most likely had about 70 pounds of pressure in it instead of the 100 or so that I had been told to put in. I pumped up the back tire about the same and that was going to have to do.

Just minutes later we were called to the swim start.

It was surreal. There were hundreds of spectators lining the sea-wall that ringed the harbor area and four television helicopters hovered above Kailua Bay. Apart from the sound of their rotors, there was an eerie silence as a priest gave a blessing for the athletes and the event that was about to take place.

The anthem followed and seconds after it was over the start gun sounded and the 1984 Hawaii Ironman was underway. My heart was pounding as I dove into the water and my two year journey to reach the Ironman finish line had reached the final stage.

2

I should mention from the very beginning that if you are an accomplished runner, a great swimmer, or good at any sport for that matter, it's best to leave your ego at home if you are taking on your first Ironman Triathlon.

I found out early on that the Ironman is the great equalizer and on a whim can crush even the best of the pro athletes if they don't show it proper respect.

When that gun went off and I dove into the warm waters of the Bay on October 6, 1984 I could not possibly have been more out of my element. It was one thing to push myself to swim two miles in a pool back home, but it was another completely to be trying to swim 2.4 miles in the open water with 1100 other people all trying to do the same thing.

It wouldn't matter if there were 5000 people in the water with you and half of them were your friends, when the gun goes off for an Ironman swim start you could not possibly be any more alone.

I really have to give Chip credit before I go any further. When I hit that water it was simply incredible how I seemed to slip through the surf. Who would have thought that simply shaving that hair off would make such a difference? For the first time I truly realized why fish have no hair.

Still it was like I was in a foreign world. Almost immediately I realized that I would have to breathe completely different in the ocean as I had learned to do in the pool. The ocean swells threw off my breathing rhythm and I swallowed so much water that I had to learn on the fly to turn my head upward much further in order to breathe air that was not laced with salt water.

Of course I had no plan going into the swim and just went into the water with the rest of the pack. That was my first mistake. It was one thing to be struggling to stay afloat, but it was another thing altogether to do it while getting bashed around by flailing arms, legs, and bodies for what seemed like an eternity.

I didn't know how to tread water so my only alternative was to keep going forward. I sure as Hell couldn't turn around and go back. I was pretty sure I would be in serious trouble if I didn't keep moving. It gave new meaning to the words *sink or swim*.

I just kept moving my arms as fast as I could and tried to find a patch of water that was not full of swimmers. I'm sure my heart-rate was skyrocketing. The fear of the water I thought I had overcome returned and I struggled to resist the urge to panic.

Then not a moment too soon I found myself in the relative calm to the left of the main pack. My erratic swimming and crappy swim stroke and pulled me to the left and it was the best thing that could have happened and what would ultimately be my savior.

It was probably 30 minutes into the swim before I began to calm down a bit and settle into some sort of constant rhythm and pushed on toward the turn against the current that was working against us. I was finally relaxed enough to spot the big orange markers to my right as they passed by and tried to key on them and stay on a straight line to the turn.

For the first time since the start gun had sounded I was able to take in this fascinating new world I found myself in.

The water was crystal clear and even this far out from shore you could see the ocean floor. There were the amazing schools of fish. Thousands of red, green, yellow, and blue schools of tropical fish weaving back and forth in swirling synchronization in front of my eyes.

Then there were the scuba divers. They were the safety net for the swim and were watching the action from below. Some even held signs up urging on local athletes.

After what seemed like forever I could see the bright orange sails of the Captain Bean boat at the turn-around. They kept getting bigger

Ray Fauteux

and bigger and I aimed for the boat and when I got there caught glimpses of people hanging over the railing urging the swimmers on.

Finally I reached the far side of the boat and the last marker that indicated the first right hand turn and the end of the outward leg of the swim. As I made the turn I was startled to see a scuba diver with an underwater camera taking pictures of the swimmers as they passed by above him.

It was a short swim to the next right hand turn and the final long leg home. Just as I had at the start, I moved my arms as fast as I could. My heart had been racing since the gun went off and I was bleeding energy.

As I made the turn I could almost feel the current lift me and push me shore ward. It was so amazing. It was at that moment that realized I was going to get this done. I could feel a rush of adrenaline as I pushed toward the finish line with my swim stroke from Hell. It was one of those moments that you remember forever.

The sun was rising to our right and bright rays glistened on the surface of the water. It didn't seem possible but it made the whole swim experience even more surreal than it already was.

Up ahead I saw the biggest can of beer I'd ever seen in my life. It was also the one can of beer I would appreciate above all others and that's saying something.

Bud Light as a major sponsor had this inflated can of beer at the swim finish line. Talk about brilliant marketing. Every single swimmer struggling to get to shore became big fans of Bud Light Beer because it was showing us the way to the finish of the swim that never seemed to end.

That inflated can of Bud got bigger and bigger by the moment and up ahead I could see swimmers being lifted up out of the water as they reached the finish ramp of the swim. Within minutes I was there and as a pair of volunteers help me get to my feet I just knew that I was going to become an Ironman that day if only my $400 hunk of steel bike with the soft tires didn't let me down.

I felt the day was already a victory for me in many ways and I was overwhelmed with a feeling of gratitude that my life had brought me here and allowed me to be part of something so incredibly special.

The scene in the transition tent is something I will never forget. It seemed like a hundred people were all talking at the same time. It was simply euphoric. Nobody seemed to be in an all out rush to leave and get on their bikes and when I think back on it, I believe there was only one reason for this.

Like myself, the Ironman swim was what seemed to worry most novice Ironman triathletes the most. In 1984 you could be quite certain that 75% and probably more of the entries in the race were first-timers. I mean the race was so new it could hardly be any other way.

That meant there were some pretty relieved and happy people in the transition tent that day. It was then that I truly realized just how special the day was going to be.

There were people there from many countries, but we were all sharing the same journey and that was what formed a special bond that would become the hallmark of every single Ironman Triathlon in the world even decades after the event was born.

So after surviving the 2.4 mile swim that even some team-mates were afraid might be my undoing in 1:38:44, the 112 mile bike leg of the Ironman lay ahead.

I had no idea that as difficult a challenge as the swim was for me, the real test was yet to come.

Ray Fauteux

3

When I went over to the bike rack to get on my bike, I half expected at least one of the tires to be flat. It was quite a relief to see they were just as I had left them before the swim. They may have been seriously under-inflated but at least I was still in the race.

It was pretty exciting leaving Kona and heading out toward the King K. Highway. The streets were lined with cheering people. It was uphill leaving town and I was standing up on the pedals going as fast as I could, almost as if I knew what I was doing.

Of course I didn't, but much like my first marathon, I just went out about as fast as I could go. Maintaining a steady pace and keeping the heart-rate as level and as low as possible were concepts that were still foreign to me. Besides, with the excitement of the moment it was pretty difficult not to get carried away.

However it wouldn't be long before the crushing heat and unforgiving winds blowing off the ocean would temper my enthusiasm. Even for Kona, the heat that day was epic. The Queen K. Highway is lined with black lava rock that draws the heat and as the sun rose in the sky the thermostat was edging up toward 108 degrees as the race progressed.

As the day wore on we cycled into shimmering heat waves that seemed like they were 6 feet off the highway. Of course without clip-less pedals we had to use toe-clips and mine didn't fit properly to start with. As the temperature rose my feet began to swell and the pain with each pedal stroke was unlike anything I'd ever experienced.

The hotter it became, the softer the asphalt seem to get and when I looked down it seemed like my soft, under-inflated tires were sinking into the road. At about the 50k mark I had biked about as far as I had ever gone in training. Physically I was pretty well finished as the energy-sapping swim and oppressive heat took it's toll.

Yet I still had 130k more to bike and a marathon to finish.

What kept me going was the image I had of the finish line. It was what had sustained me through all the months of learning how to swim and it sustained me out on the bike course. As the day wore on, I began to see more and more bikes stopped on the side of the road. Ambulances screamed up and down the highway. The wind never seemed to be a tail-wind and was relentless.

After what seemed like an eternity I found myself at the foot of the climb to Hawi and the turn-around point of the bike course. I started up the hill and the wind was horrific and was hitting us from the side as it howled off the ocean and I was barely able to keep the forward momentum going, but was managing to hang on. There was nowhere to hide from it and aero-bars had still not been invented so we were at the mercy of the wind.

The lead cyclists came tearing down the hill with motorcycles leading the way. Pro Ironmen named John Howard, Mark Allen, and Dave Scott went roaring by like freight trains.

Up ahead I saw another cyclist weaving back and forth. He was in big trouble and as I watched the wind blew him right over onto his side. I knew as I struggled past him that it would be pretty well impossible for him to get back on his bike on the incline and he would have to push his bike the rest of the way up the hill if he hoped to continue on in the race.

I couldn't believe it when I finally reached the crest of the hill and made it to the turn-around. For the first time I was able to rest a little as I went down the hill I had just climbed. I thought for sure that the wind that had been against us for so long would be at our backs, but when I reached the bottom of the hill it was as bad as it was when I was going the other direction. That's mostly because it wasn't a true headwind, but was coming at us from the side and howling in from the ocean.

I was into my fourth hour of biking and at about the second hour I had wanted to stop and lay down on the side of the road. The only consolation now was that I was on the return journey and half way

Ray Fauteux

back to the run transition and the waiting marathon.

I began to have trouble holding my head up so I could see ahead and a great weariness enveloped me. I didn't think it was possible, but I actually felt like I was going to fall asleep at the wheel, or I guess I should say, wheels. Up ahead I saw what I thought was a hallucination. As I got closer and closer it looked like it was a beautiful Hawaiian girl in a grass skirt with flowers in her hair.

Well, it really "was" a beautiful Hawaiian girl in a grass skirt. She was all alone at this table on the side of the highway holding something out to me. I could have sworn–or perhaps I hoped–it was a cool sponge that would be heavenly in the blistering heat. I pulled myself together and swooped in like I was Dave Scott leading the race and snatched that guava jelly sandwich on brown bread from her small fingers and smashed it against the back of my neck.

An instant before it hit I realized it was not a sponge, but it happened pretty fast and the dizzying heat did little to speed up my reaction time. I have a feeling that many strange things happened out on the Ironman course that day as many of us struggled to survive and resist the urge to simply stop and give up.

The miles seemed to pass by so slowly and once in a while I would catch up to someone who was going even slower than I was, but most of the time I was the one who was being passed. I wondered how everyone else from Calgary was doing and as yet had not seen any of them. Of course in my state they could have biked right past me and I wouldn't have realized it anyway.

Finally off to the right I could see the airport we had arrived at two weeks earlier. That meant I was closing in on Kona and it lifted my spirits and gave me a burst of energy that took me closer and closer to town.

Every once in a while another ambulance would go screaming by or I would see a van picking up a dejected cyclist who's day had come to an end. It was sad to see because they were so close to Kona. But I can certainly understand where it can be pretty over-whelming to feel like crap and in the back of your mind realize there was still a marathon to run.

I thought back to when I watched Julie Moss collapse on TV at the finish line of the 1982 Ironman and now I understood how easily that could happen. It was happening to people right in front of my eyes even before they reached the bike/run transition.

I finally rolled into town and the shade of the buildings and the welcome downhill leading to Ali'i Drive provided momentary relief but we still had to bike out of the other side of town, past the Sea Village where we were staying, and over to a hotel that was at the bottom of a steep hill. It was appropriately called "the pit" and that was where the final transition would be.

Finally I made the last left-hand turn to the road leading to the bike transition. You might say being able to coast down the big hill into the transition area was a reward for enduring the Hell that was the Queen K. Highway, but it really wasn't because running up the damn hill would be the start of the marathon.

As much as I had about enough of my bike to last a life-time I had to admit that it was pretty amazing that the severely under-inflated tires never gave out and that my $400 bike had held together for 112 miles. Strange as it may seem I felt very connected to that bike. It was as if we had just gone to war together and had barely managed to survive. Thinking back on it, that's not far from the truth.

As I finally rolled to a stop about four volunteers caught the bike. I think they had discovered from earlier arrivals that many riders were simply unable to get off their bikes without help.

7 hours, 38 minutes and 56 seconds had passed since I had left the Kona pier at the beginning of the bike leg. I can't find the words to describe how amazingly difficult it was to get off that bike and try to walk. Everything that could possibly hurt did hurt. I had never felt so stiff and I just couldn't see how it would be possible to get out there and face another 26.2 miles of Hell.

I went into the change tent and it was a far different atmosphere

Ray Fauteux

than the euphoria of the transition tent at the end of the swim. This time it was more like a mash unit on steroids. Still, the guys that were in there just sort of looked at each other and nodded, because despite everything we had made it this far in this journey called *Ironman*.

It was about 10 minutes before I could make myself leave that tent and begin the final 26.2 mile stage. The climb out of the pit was brutal but in many ways it helped me get into a body rhythm that was far different from being on the bike.

There were many other factors at play now. Like almost everyone in the race I was most likely dehydrated and had not taken on nearly enough water. Chances are I never ate enough either. It was my own fault.

I should have eaten that guava jelly sandwich.

For a while it actually didn't feel too bad once my body began to loosen up and I was able to run slowly back toward Kona. As I made my way through town and back to the searing King K. Highway the thousands of cheering spectators provided a much needed mental and emotional boost and I will never forget them and how much they meant to all of us who were part of the Ironman that day.

I would like to take a moment and say that I was quite proud that I passed Dave Scott as I was leaving Kona behind. Oh, did I mention that we passed going in opposite directions? I was just getting to the top of the hill when I saw Dave running towards me toward the finish line. He had decimated the field and would cross the finish line over twenty minutes ahead of second place finisher Scott Tinley.

The uphill leaving Kona was my undoing and whatever energy I had left deserted me after just a few miles out on the King K. Highway. I just wanted to die. I wanted to stop and lay down on the side of the road.

I had to be careful though. You could feel that way and think that way, but there were medical staff traveling up and down the highway and their word was law. If they decided to pull you from the course your race was over despite all that you had endured to that point.

It became a death march.

It was run-walk, run-walk, and with the airport in sight once again it was walk and shuffle any way you could. The airport meant that the final turn-around was near. They had this little structure built in the middle of the highway and you ran in one side and turned, and then ran out the other side.

So in the sudden darkness of the tropic night, reaching the finish line would come down to how badly you wanted it. Not just for me, but for all the warriors, male and female left standing as the final push for home began.

4

The images, sounds, and sometimes eerie silence of those last desperate miles are burned into my memory and will stay with me forever.

I think you really had to be there to understand how absolutely heart-breaking it was to be struggling along the highway and come across someone laying on the side of the road totally spent and not capable of taking one more step. To come so far only to be taken the rest of the way in an ambulance would be devastating.

"There but for the grace of God go I."

I kept thinking that over and over and despite everything I felt blessed that I was able to keep moving on into the night.

It was only the light from the moon that kept us from being in total darkness. Later I was to learn that the date for the Ironman was set in order to have a full moon light the highway for the run. I can't say for sure if it's true or not, but it makes perfect sense.

Even so it was still quite dark and then something really special happened. It caught me by surprise because the only time I had ever run at night was in the 50 mile road race that started at midnight a few years back.

As night cloaked the Queen K. Highway volunteers started handing out light-sticks. They had a green-yellow glow and I had never seen anything quite so visually amazing in any race.

The lights stretched out for miles along the highway and for the first time you could see how many other triathletes were winding their way along the highway. The vibrant lights moved in all different directions as people had them tucked in their head-bands, shorts or held them in their hands and swung them up and down as they ran, shuffled, or walked.

On and on it went, the highway with no end and then I saw a faint glow on the horizon and I felt my heart lift and hope begin to seep into my thoughts.

It was the lights of Kona! What an amazing feeling it was to finally have the end of this amazing journey in sight.

Often in life we feel we can go no further, we can do no more, and that one more step is impossible. In that one moment we face the abyss, the ultimate challenge of mind, body, and spirit and discover an inner strength we never knew existed and in a glorious revelation realize that our lives are about to change forever.

And that's exactly what was about to happen.

It is a strange phenomenon of endurance events that for some reason you can feel like death for so long, but if you can just hang in there you often get a second wind and an injection of strength and you wonder where the Hell it has been all day.

With about three miles to go I started to run as well as I had at any time over the marathon course. It wasn't fast, but it was steady and with each passing minute the lights of Kona were getting brighter and brighter.

Finally after almost 14 hours out on that race course I saw someone else from the Try-Ten Team. It was Chip the belly-flopping beach bum and Pierre another one of the guys and they were running together. Or I should say, *shuffling* together.

I think the reason it even registered with me was because Chip was so big and it was hard to miss his silhouette in the light of the moon. They were both staring down at the road about 3 feet in front of them and I could tell that every ounce of their strength and concentration was going into each step.

To this day they don't know that I passed them that night. I never said anything. I believe that instinctively I thought it would harm what rhythm they had and I just carried on and passed within a foot of them and they never even noticed me so yes, they were as out of it as I was.

Ray Fauteux

Even after the race–years after the race–I never said anything. This is the first time, in this book that I have mentioned it. It's not a big deal but it was one of many moments that took place that day and night that have stayed with me over the years.

It was getting really exciting right around then. You could make out the outlines of buildings now as Kona drew closer and closer. More and more spectators were lining the road. I came to the final aid station and there must have been 15 volunteers handing out water for the final run to the finish line.

And holy crap! Two of them were the evil sisters from Winnipeg!

"Hey!" I called out as I ran right through the aid station and they both started jumping up and down and screaming.

The whole experience became very surreal as I reached the streets of town and I was running with more conviction than I had in the entire marathon since staggering out of the pit back at the bike transition. Hundreds and hundreds of people were on the sidewalks of the town cheering.

It was a glorious downhill run to Ali'i Drive and I could smell the ocean in the breeze and knew the seawall and the finish line were coming up fast.

I took time to look behind me and couldn't see anyone. I looked ahead and I couldn't see anyone. In one of those strange quirks of that long, long day, it seemed that I was all alone on the course.

Cool.

I could finally make out the sea-wall and knew there was just one right hand turn left to make and I would be home.

As I was approaching it, I had the strangest feeling. In those last few moments as I reached the turn it was as if everything was in slow motion. What had started out as an almost impossible dream some two years ago, was moments away from becoming a reality.

In fact you could go back six more years before that when I was sitting in the car the night of my very first struggling run and for a moment had considered just giving up on my dream to *become more.*

Because I never gave in to self-doubt and the always present fear of failure, it changed me forever and the winding road of my rejuvenated life would eventually bring me to where I am today, writing this book for you.

I rounded that corner and I will never forget the sight that greeted me. There was a straight stretch of a few hundred yards to the finish line. It was a solid mass of people lining both sides of the road. Some were standing up on the sea-wall to get a better view.

Up ahead I could see big blazing lights and they were the ABC camera lights shining down on the finish line. The same lights that were shining down on Julie Moss during Ironman Hawaii 1982 when I watched her collapse just before the finish on Wide World of Sports on ABC television.

I ran towards the lights and people were shouting out "Ironman! Ironman! You're going to be an Ironman!"

There was no more pain.

The sight of the finish was the ultimate cure and through the joyful haze of tears and the fog of exhaustion I crossed the line and instinctively knew that life for me would never be quite the same again.

In that moment I was on a high that no drug could ever match and that same passion and high has remained for almost four decades and even now as I write these lines I can almost taste the salt in the air and feel the warm ocean breeze on my face.

Ray Fauteux

5

I had crossed the Ironman finish line in a time of 14:16:33. My marathon time was 4:58:53. It was a far cry from my 2:56 Marathon in Seaside, Oregon.

I think it's a good indication of the challenges the Ironman represented in the early days. There's no doubt that not having the best of equipment was a big factor for everyone. For the entire 112 miles of the Hawaii Ironman bike course my destiny rested on my $400 bike and whether or not my two under-inflated tires would hold together long enough to get me to the run transition.

As a runner, depending on anything other than myself to get me through a race was foreign to me.

When I finally made it back to my room the night of the race, I collapsed onto my bed and woke up almost exactly 8 hours later wearing the clothes I wore when I walked into my room the night before. It was remarkable. It was like 5 minutes had passed, and I don't think I even moved in my sleep and woke up exactly where I landed on the bed. Never in my life been so totally exhausted. Even more exhausted than I as after the 50-mile race.

Seven of my team-mates crossed the finish line. That was quite an amazing feat considering nine of us started as Tony had to withdraw before the race. Grant, the one member who was unable to reach the finish had bike problems and was unable to continue.

Tony would never attempt an Ironman again. He was devastated when he was unable to compete in the race.

Grant went on to complete an Ironman race in Penticton in a later year and followed his dream of being a coach and became one of the best triathlon coaches around.

Julia was amazing and made the podium by finishing 5th in her age group. I don't know what eventually became of the three very tough women from the team. I know that Dave Scott the winner of the race would come to Calgary a few months after the Ironman and stay with Julia and her husband-to-be while he visited the city on some sort of promotion.

Pierre who was running with Chip when I passed them finished three minutes behind me, and Chip finished 13 minutes behind Pierre. Chip had an amazing performance as well considering how big he was. I can only imagine how difficult the marathon must have been for him. He finished the swim in 1:03, over 35 minutes ahead of me.

The last I heard of Pierre was that he owned a bar in Key West that kept getting demolished every hurricane season. Then he had a job that had him flying all over the Caribbean as some sort of wine rep.

Chip, as I mentioned earlier, went on to create a clothing empire called LuluLemon and became a very successful businessman.

Dave Scott won the race in a time of 8:54:20. I don't even know how you equate that with the times of today. Dave never had aero-bars or clip-less pedals. His bike was not made of titanium. Yet after a 50 minute swim he finished the bike course in 5:10 and the marathon in 2:53.

He was truly far ahead of his time. It has an honor to be in the same event with him and all the other great pros who competed that day.

As an indication of how tough the conditions were, Dave was the only one in the race to break 3 hours in the marathon.

The second place finisher was Scott Tinley in a time of 9:18:45, a full 24 minutes behind Dave Scott. His marathon was 11 minutes slower than Dave's.

An Olympic swimmer named Djan Madruga was the first one out of the water in 47:48.2. Truly a spectacular performance. He would be passed later on during the bike and run by all the pros and would fall off the pace and would not place in the top five at the finish.

The Puntos twins from Montreal came in first and second for the women.

I suppose as can only be expected from identical twins, they finished the swim less than seven seconds apart. They finished the bike five seconds apart. They ran together for about 23 miles, and I suppose sisterly love ended about there and whoever had the most left would be destined to win the race.

The Winnipeg sisters had some great stories to tell because they spent the entire night at the last aid station before the finish line. They said it was so remarkable to see the athletes get so close to Kona and the finish line. They said it was so moving to see how many triathletes were just willing themselves to keep on moving toward the finish.

They saw Dave Scott come flying by followed a full 22 minutes later by Scott Tinley with his sun-bleached, pure white, California surfer-dude hair. They saw Mark Allen come by in fifth place. In later years in his career Mark would become a 6-time Ironman Hawaii Champion.

The sisters said the best part of the whole experience was when the Puntos twins arrived at their aid station. The first to arrive was Sylviane who had broken away from her sister a few miles back. They said she stopped, took a cup of water, drank half, and poured the other half over her head and kept on running into Kona and a first place finish for the women.

Not two minutes later her twin sister Patricia arrived dressed exactly the same, hair exactly the same, and running style exactly the same. She stopped, took a cup of water, drank half, and poured the other half over her head and kept on running into Kona and a second place finish for the women.

Remarkably, not only did they look exactly alike and have just about the same ability, they each did exactly the same thing at the aid station.

Sylvianne crossed the finish line in 10:25:13 and Patricia in 10:27:28.

To me the most amazing stat was that these two amazingly talented women were only 23 years old at the time. That means if they were racing today they would be kicking ass in the 60-65 age group. They would go on to compete in many more Ironman races and at one time had hopes of making the qualifying time for the 1988 Olympic Marathon in Seoul, Korea.

Of over 1100 starters, 903 finished Ironman Hawaii 1984. That was actually a very big drop out rate. It can mostly be attributed to the heat, wind, and lack of experience. Or perhaps a combination of all three.

We found out later that a drama unfolded during the swim the morning of the race. We all had identifying bracelets on and our numbers were recorded when we came out of the water. After the swim there was one swimmer unaccounted for.

Apparently scuba divers had scoured the swim course searching the floor of the Bay fearing the worst. Well it turns out that the missing swimmer had decided not to answer the staring gun. He simply got freaked out and too scared to face the swim and went across the street from the pier and had breakfast at a restaurant on the course and watched the race unfold from a patio.

It never dawned on him that he was still wearing his bracelet and nobody knew where the Hell he was. So I guess he eventually sauntered on over to the pier a few hours later to see what all the excitement was about and the mystery was solved.

I can understand completely the fear he felt at the start of the swim, because I had been there myself and had to will myself to answer the starting gun.

As I mentioned earlier, for many years it would be the hottest Ironman races on record with temperatures hovering over the 110 degree mark out on the sweltering Queen K. Highway.

The awards dinner was Sunday night and by Monday 1100 triathletes started to make their way home.

Ray Fauteux

Hell not me. I was a single guy in Hawaii and I headed for Oahu for a week to celebrate.

6

It was the best of days and the high I was on from the Ironman put me on cloud nine and no matter what I did in Oahu it turned out just about perfect.

For starters I had thrown out the cardboard bike box I had used for the original flight to Hawaii and just checked my bike in as it was when I left Kona. When I arrived in Oahu my bike was just fine when I claimed it along with my other luggage. Pretty much everyone was on pins and needles about their bike getting damaged in transit.

I stuck most of my luggage into a storage locker at the airport and walked out of the terminal with a backpack and my bike and was wearing my Ironman *finisher* t-shirt. I asked this lady cop how to get to Kaheo Avenue because that's where my hotel was. She pointed me to the highway and said "follow that road," so off I went.

The first thing I saw on the highway was a "no bikes allowed" sign.

What the Hell?

Well I assumed that it was a sign that nobody really payed much attention to because it was a cop who pointed me in this direction and she could hardly have missed my bike.

There was a time when I would have caved in and just headed back and taken a taxi into town, but that was then and this was now.

So there I was cycling down the freeway past Pearl Harbor when a convertible full of women went zooming past. Can you say University of Hawaii?

As they passed me when one of them turned around and shouted "we love Ironmen!"

Holy crap! I guess they saw the bike and the t-shirt and put two and

Ray Fauteux

two together. Who knows, maybe they had been in Kona as spectators or volunteers. Regardless, it was pretty cool.

So I get to the Royal Kaheo Hotel and roll my bike on into the lobby and check in. I mean this was a pretty good hotel and I half expected them to say, "you can't take that bike up to your room!"

No problem. The girl behind the desk just looked at me and looked at my bike and saw that we had this thing going on and didn't say a word except for "enjoy your stay".

So what does a single Ironman do when he's all alone in the romance capital of the world? Well, I guess he better find himself some female companionship to make this amazing three weeks complete.

So I go up to this *entertainment floor* of the hotel as they called it, and found that it had everything. There were barbecues, ping pong tables, a pool, and a drop-dead gorgeous, petite, blonde girl in a bikini all by herself reading a book.

So I just walked on over and said "Hi!"

That in itself was totally out of character for me.

I was instantly attracted to this gorgeous woman with the ready smile and she was just as easy to talk to as she was to look at.

It turns out that beautiful Kathy was from Vancouver and she was on a Hawaiian holiday with her sister and a girlfriend.

Yes, there is a God was my first thought.

We made small talk for a few minutes and when she asked me about myself I just sort of blurted out, "I'm here by myself and I was just in Kona and was in the Ironman Triathlon would you like to go out for dinner with me tonight?"

It sort of came out all in one long sentence.

Well, why beat around the bush. I figured the worst she could say was no. When I think back it was actually pretty funny. No sir, no mincing words here.

To her credit, she never batted an eye. "Sure" she said, "I'd love to," and I fell instantly in love.

So that evening I met her in the lobby of the hotel and we taxied on over to this fabulous restaurant that one of the bellhops had suggested. I told him I needed to find a special place for a special girl.

It was called Bobby Mcgee's and it was simply amazing. Everyone who worked there was dressed up in stunning costumes. "Merlin the Magician" came over to the table and did some card tricks for us as we waited for our meal. "Little Bo Peep" and "Snow White" served us and they were two very beautiful Hawaiian girls.

The food, the wine, and the company were all pretty sensational that night.

After dinner Kathy suggested we forego the taxi and walk the mile or so back along the beach to the hotel.

Oh....all right.

We were about half-way back to the hotel when we stopped and I held her and I gazed into those amazing blue eyes and at her long, silky blonde hair that framed her impish smile. There are really no words that can do justice to that moment in time.

The sky was filled with stars and rolling waves thundered against the shore as moonbeams danced and sparkled on the ocean surface for as far as the eye could see.

Over the years I have come to believe that a fulfilling and happy life is not necessarily measured by the amount of breaths we take, but rather by the moments that take out breath away.

When you think about it, much of what happens in our lives is lost in the din and the fog of everyday life. Often it's when we step

Ray Fauteux

aside from the monotonous sameness and challenge ourselves to become more that we truly begin to *live*.

There was a day when I never would have had the courage to approach someone as amazing as Kathy let alone ask her out to dinner. Like most people the fear of being turned down–the fear of failure in all things–often caused me to hesitate.

In that singular moment of doubt the opportunity can be lost forever, never to return.

There is no doubt in my mind that it was my Ironman journey and the end result had instilled confidence in me that I once lacked. Even had Kathy said "no" it would not have been at all devastating. By then I knew what I was truly capable of and how much promise life had in store for me if I continued to believe in myself despite all the setbacks that life threw in my path.

As I have told people over and over in person and in the books I write, once you start believing in yourself and gain self-confidence it can potentially open up a whole new world.

It doesn't matter what it is that energizes your life and your belief in yourself. It can be just going out and challenging yourself to get fit, lose weight, run your first 10k race, take a new career path, start a meaningful relationship, or become a triathlete and one day cross the Ironman finish line.

Whenever you face any challenge that tests your limits on any number of levels and you succeed and overcome adversity there is often a natural high associated with that success.

There is no drug in the world capable of sustaining the high I have been on for almost four decades since discovering that there is a whole world of possibilities out there waiting for each of us.

I felt so alive by the time I arrived in Oahu from Kona that I felt there was nothing I couldn't do. It was a special time and I simply wanted to share it with someone and it turned out to be an amazing woman who at another time in my life, I never would have had the confidence to approach.

I shared my story about Kathy because I just wanted to illustrate how believing in yourself and stretching the boundaries of your capabilities and achieving things that once seemed impossible, change not only the way you feel about yourself, but also the way other people perceive you. Suddenly I exuded a self-confidence and bravado that for so long had been foreign to me.

Over the years I have come to realize that the Ironman far exceeds an athletic endurance event. It offers the possibility for so many people to be so much more. It is an opportunity for positive growth and change in about every way imaginable because it has a way of bringing so many previously hidden qualities to life.

What a shame that so many people will live their entire lives and not realize their true potential, especially when it's just waiting to be discovered and is within their grasp and they simply don't realize it. Life has so much to offer if we are willing to take a leap of faith and reach out for it.

The rest of the week in Oahu flew by and far too soon I was saying a last goodbye to Kathy and winging my way back to Calgary.

We wrote back and forth for months until one day she got engaged and over the years we lost touch as people tend to do. Whenever I think back to that special time in Hawaii in 1984, that magical evening with Kathy is always foremost in my thoughts.

Others from the Try Ten Team were on the same flight back home and all of them were packing their bikes around in bike boxes. I stuck my trusty bike into a taxi-van just the way it was on race day for the trip to the airport. Pretty much all of them said my bike would be crushed by the time we got home.

When I checked in at the airport the girl looked at me and looked at the bike and could see what we had this thing going and said "have a nice flight" and took my bike from me. No extra charge, no removing the pedals, wheels, and handle-bars and no lecture. Just a smile and "have a nice flight".

When the girls serving us on the plane heard we had been in the Ironman the free drinks on that nearly empty huge Jumbo 747 began to flow. Especially when one of them asked me if she could have an Ironman t-shirt.

Oh...all right.

But she would have to wait until we got to Calgary because they were in my checked luggage..

I have to say that when we picked up our race packages in Kona before the race it was quite a pleasant surprise. The race organizers had gone all out to make the event special. Our race bags contained three Ironman Hawaii t-shirts and the silky red, white, and blue singlet and short set that were worn by the U.S. Olympic team at the Games in Los Angeles that year. Plus I had my finisher T-shirt.

So I thought what the Hell, what would it hurt to give one to her.

Well at the time I was drinking Grand Marnier with my coffee and soon she was bringing me 3 ounce glasses of the stuff and it just never stopped coming. I thought that any minute she was just going to bring the entire bottle over and plunk it down on my tray. She really wanted that t-shirt.

It was quite the trip home.

When we arrived at the airport and stood waiting by the luggage carousel everyone sort of wondered if my bike would be a pile of crushed metal and rubber. I was the only one who didn't spend two hours taking my bike apart and packing it into a bike box.

Well it wasn't on the carousel and when I turned around, there it was in all it's glory leaning against a post in perfect condition. The little bike that could had survived once again.

As I pulled my suitcase off the conveyor belt, it never even hit the floor and the flight attendant from the plane was standing behind me waiting for the t-shirt I had promised her. I pulled out this red muscle shirt that had Ironman Hawaii 1984 all over it and handed it to her.

She was so happy that she gave me this big kiss and to the this day I still sort of wish I had kept that shirt, but on the other hand it was special to share the experience with someone in some small way.

So on that note, my great Hawaii Ironman adventure ended and it was back home and back to reality with plenty to think about and many decisions to make.

Ray Fauteux

IRON AMBITIONS

I had this huge walk-in storage room in my apartment and the first thing I did when I got home from the airport was open the storage room door and shove my bike in.

It's hard to describe the feelings I had after returning home from my Ironman adventure. When I began to come down emotionally from all that had transpired over the previous few weeks I had an overwhelming sense of tiredness. Of course there would have to be recovery time from the physical stress, but it was more than that.

There is an emotional and mental drain as well when you push yourself to the limit of your endurance and I also believe there is a chemical imbalance caused by all the different stresses. I think that goes a long way toward explaining why many people--especially those who do their *first* Ironman--go through a bit of a depression in the weeks and months following the event.

Getting over the aches and pains is just one part of the recovery process and I decided I would ease off on training of any kind for a while and take some time to decide what I wanted to do as far as triathlon was concerned. I instinctively felt it would not be too wise to make a hasty decision and I should wait until I was fully recovered.

Come to think of it, several finishers of the Ironman that year in Hawaii sold their bikes before they even left Kona. They made up their minds right away that they would never do another Ironman. It was a natural reaction because of what they had just endured, but I often think about that and hope they were not to hasty in their decision.

Over the years I would encounter many people who just wanted to cross the Ironman finish line once and then call it a career. That's different.

They know going in and they have a plan. It's as if becoming an

Ironman is on their *to do list* as something they wanted to accomplish sometime in their life and then cross it off the list once it was done.

There's not a thing wrong with that. Once you cross the Ironman finish line just once you are an Ironman for life and nobody can take that away from you. As for myself, I had plenty to think about over the following weeks and months.

Running had been a huge challenge for me until I reached the point after six years or so that I had accomplished all I thought I was capable of in the sport.

Running was no longer enough. I knew that.

I was driven to strive for more of a challenge and when I had first heard the call of the Ironman in 1982 the timing was perfect. Now it was a matter of deciding what I was going to do next.

I gave it plenty of thought and decided my main focus would be on the Ironman. It would be seven months later in June of 1985 when I finally brought the bike back out of the closet.

Believe it or not there was still some air left in the tires. My race number was still attached to the bike and sweat stains and remnants of dried guava jelly sandwich adorned the frame. Memories came flooding back but it was the memory of crossing the finish line in Kona that day was foremost in my thoughts.

That was more than enough to inspire me to attempt to live the Ironman experience again.

I attempted a few of the local triathlons that were just beginning to make an appearance around Alberta. It was a disaster. Without a wetsuit and being so low in body fat the cold water simply made it impossible for me to enjoy the events as I would always struggle in the cold water.

After those first few initial attempts I would only compete in one more triathlon in my Province and it was about 15 years into my career. It was the Great White North Triathlon in Stoney Plain, Alberta and it was and still is an amazing triathlon. Also by then, wetsuit technology had evolved and cold water was not as much of a factor.

Regardless, I would never train in the open water and did all my training in the pool. The only time I would swim in the open water apart from that one race would be on Ironman race day.

Ironman Hawaii 1985 came and went and five months before the 1986 race I decided I would go back to Kona.

I spent hours and hours trying to become a better swimmer and biked further and further now that I knew what to expect. Aero-bars and clip-less pedals were on the market and I had them put on my bike.

I booked another 3-week holiday, spent thousands of dollars on gear flight, and accommodations and trained for months to become a better triathlete. This time I didn't intend to just survive the Ironman but wanted to really improve on my first attempt.

Little did I know how this trip was going to play out and I learned just how fickle and unpredictable the journey to the Ironman start line can be.

2

This time I made the trip to Kona alone as the rest of the Try-Ten Team had all taken their lives in different directions. Some would never do another triathlon, and some like myself were destined to have a long career in the sport.

Once again I stayed at the Sea Village and met more really great people from all over the world and ended up hanging out with this very friendly couple from Adelaide, South Australia and Pam from San Diego who was in Kona on holidays. I had asked Kevan from the Bike Shop if he wanted to come out and stay as a guest in my condo because of the all the help he had given me with my bike.

So Kevan came out to watch the Ironman and together with my new Australian and American friends we went to the spectacular pre-race dinner at a 5-star hotel in Kona.

They had incredible food and I tried everything and it was at that dinner that I made a mistake that would have a devastating impact my entire experience in Kona in 1986.

There were only two things that I really had to avoid eating because of the allergic reaction they caused. It was clams and oysters and without thinking I had some pasta with clam sauce from one of the food stations. At first I had no idea it was clam sauce and by the time I realized it, it was too late.

From that time on until the start of the race I was sick. I still decided to at least try on race day and made it to the turn on the swim course and to within site of the swim finish but I was just too sick to carry on and was pulled from the course by the medical staff.

As I said before, the medical staff has the final say and there is no recourse. I had been throwing up on and off for over a mile and felt like death. If you combine that with the up and down motion of the ocean swells, you can imagine what it was like. They don't take people off the Ironman course lightly because they realize how much effort people have put into just getting there.

Their feeling was that I would simply be to dehydrated to be out in the heat of the Queen K. Highway. They were right of course, and Ironman Hawaii 1986 was over for me.

If it had been my first Ironman I'm sure I would have been devastated but because I had reached the finish line in 1984 I was more able to take it in stride. I learned from the experience and still loved the Ironman atmosphere and enjoyed every minute of my time in Kona.

As I said in the very beginning of this book, if you want to truly motivate and inspire people you have to be willing to share the good and the bad, because there will always be stumbling blocks in life that will test us and that in essence is what makes future success that much sweeter.

It was these obstacles and shortcomings that would be the cornerstone of the Ironstruck books I would write in the years to come. Through my experiences both good and bad I would be able to help thousands of others learn and avoid the same fate and inspire them to begin their own journey and reach their own distant finish lines.

I learned some very big lessons on that trip. First of all I learned that you can do 30 Ironman races and if you show any weakness at all or lose respect for the Ironman, the Iron Gods can crush you like a bug if you think you have become bigger than the race.

To me one of the most endearing qualities of the Ironman is that it can continually humble you and will always demand respect and in doing so encourages you to be at your very best on any given race day.

Was I discouraged by the outcome of Ironman Hawaii 1986? No. Actually it was exactly the opposite.

I became more determined than ever because I had found a

challenge that to this point surpassed anything I had ever encountered and the Ironman would dictate course of my life for a long, long time.

Ray Fauteux

3

Ironman Canada in Penticton was beginning to grow in popularity and two years would pass before I would make this race my next objective.

In 1988 I began what would become a ritual for the next seven years. I would train all year, enter Ironman Canada, sign up for the next year, and then train all year again for the next race. Basically it was seven years of trying to figure the Ironman out and trying to understand what it would take to actually get better and finish faster.

For many people who follow the Ironman trail for years, there seems to be a natural progression. The first race you just want to survive and reach the finish line. The second race you want to take what you learned from the first race and have a better result, or at least manage the course with less physical and mental stress because you sort of now what to expect.

From there many triathletes set their sights on being the best in their age group. Some become so successful they become pros. Some just go to enjoy the race year after year and love being part of the Ironman experience and all that it encompasses and aren't concerned with how long it takes to get to the finish line.

For me, enjoying the Ironman became the unrelenting drive to reach the Ironman finish line as fast as I could and one day hopefully make it to a top five finish in my age-group and make the podium.

In 1988 in Penticton I had the race I thought I could've had in Kona in 1986 had things turned out differently. My swim time was almost an identical time as my first race in Kona but I was almost an hour faster in both the bike and run and finished in a time of 12:20:13. In 1989 I followed it up with a time of 12:23. I seemed to have found the limit of my capability as far as the Ironman, but I was wrong.

It was the year after the Calgary Winter Olympic Games when an unexpected opportunity came along that would serve as a departure from the rigors of endless, swimming, biking, and running and ultimately take my endurance to a whole new level.

Someone told me about this wild sport that a few crazies were doing over at the bobsled run at Canada Olympic Park. I soon as he said "crazies" I knew I had to go check it out.

So one night I found myself over at the bobsled track to check it out. There was a viewing area where you could watch the action from. I couldn't believe it when I say this sled come roaring down the track with this guy laying in his stomach and his nose about 3 inches from the ice.

I think my mouth was open when he disappeared into the 260 degree turn and was pinned up on the ice-wall. I would learn later that the G-force was about a five, or the equivalent of a shuttle take-off.

What I was watching was a skeleton come down the track and of course had no idea what the Hell it was because it was a basically a Winter sport that was very popular in Europe, but because it was not yet an Olympic sport nobody in Canada really knew much about it. Besides, until the Calgary Olympics the only bobsled track in North America was in Lake Placid.

I knew right away I had to try this and was soon taking the elementary instruction and made my first one run down from the luge start about half-way up the track. It was amazing, and the best was yet to come because the real start line was at the very top where the bobsleds started.

When I stood at the top of the run the night of my first official skeleton run looking out over the lights of Calgary, I was experiencing something in between sheer terror and indescribable exhilaration. They didn't even let us take a running start because it would have been way too fast and we lay down on the skeleton and were given a gentle nudge to get us started.

The turns came at me so fast that it looked like I was sliding into a solid wall, but the sled would whip around the corner in the blink of an eye and left me breathless. After every turn I picked up more speed and by the time I was at the straight-away about half-way down I was doing around 80 kph. That was without a running start.

I couldn't quite keep my head up in the 260 degree turn when the centrifugal force pushed it toward the ice and burned the end of my nose. Almost all the rookies had the same problem and it was because you had to develop neck strength in order to keep your head up, or do the really smart thing and get a helmet with a face guard.

Go figure.

Well, it was a ritual. They never told us because it was part of the indoctrination I guess and everyone had a good laugh at all the rookies with the end of their nose bleeding from skimming across the ice.

For two years I would fly down that ice three times a week and three times a night. They would limit us to three runs because the g-forces were too hard on the body. Soon I as hitting closer to 90k an hour or more depending on the ice conditions.

In 1990 I went down the bobsled run over 125 times, probably more than anyone in the country including the Olympic bob-sled team. I never missed a night and like everything else I did, it was full speed ahead and completely compulsive by nature.

Of those 125 runs I crashed about 30 times before finally figuring out turns six, seven, and eight that were called Omega. Early on I would be bruised from my shoulders to my wrists from hitting the ice walls until I learned the proper place to have padding to absorb the impact.

It was a frustrating sport because ultimately, the steel runners you have on your sled are what will most often determine how fast your run times will be. At the end of my second year I came within a whisker of making it into a world cup. I had the wrong runners on my sled for the conditions of the day and they were simply too slow. That day was my final run down the track at Canada Olympic Park.

I felt that I had taken it as far as I could and it was time to get back to the Ironman, because I felt my best race was yet to come and so the challenge was still their to motivate me.

The two years I spent on skeleton had forced me to take time off from the rigors of running, swimming, and biking and it was a blessing in disguise. It was also during that time that a luger told me about a diet I should try that would increase my endurance.

It was a diet created by a Dr. Robert Haas called the "Eat To Win" diet.

I can't help but think it was these two factors, this new diet and taking time off triathlon training that impacted my future race performance in a way that caught me completely by surprise.

Ray Fauteux

4

I always maintained a passion for running and all throughout my triathlon career I was running marathons and 10k races on a regular basis. I was actually incorporating them into my Ironman training. I unexpectedly started to have excellent race results running even though my main focus was on the Ironman.

I was sticking to the Eat To Win diet religiously, but it also dawned on me at the time that I was running far, far less than I had in the past, yet at 40 years old was running as fast as I had at 28 when I set personal bests that I had never managed to better in almost 15 years.

I had run several 10k races in sub-36 minute time when I found myself at the start line of the Calgary Marathon on July 8, 1990. It was billed as the Canadian Marathon Championships and there were many really good runners in the field. I was running in the 40-44 age group.

The strange thing was that I had no pre-conceived goals as far as this marathon went. Basically it was a training run for me in preparation for Ironman Canada in August, 1990 about 7 weeks later. When the gun sounded for the marathon I took off near the front as I always did. I usually did this just so I wouldn't get behind a few hundred slower runners at the start. If that happened it was a bit of a nuisance having to weave your way around them.

I wasn't even 2k into the race when I started to get into a ridiculous speed duel with another runner near the front. It really bugged me to have someone right behind me and I think he was drafting off me so I began to speed up to get away from him. Well he did the same thing and was right back in the same spot again, so I had to run even faster to get rid of the pest. Finally I did but the consequences of reaching the 10k mark in under 38 minutes would end up having a huge negative impact on my marathon.

I couldn't believe how effortless it seemed to maintain a really good pace despite the speed duel. I believe it was at the 30k mark when they held up projected finish times assuming one maintained the same pace for the remainder of the race. It said 2:44. Holy crap!

I was on pace to smash a personal best marathon time I set in 1977. With 5k left to go I was in 19th place and it was about there I felt myself slowing down. It was so frustrating when I was so close to an amazing time in a race I hadn't even taken seriously.

It was like slow motion when first one, than two, and than a third male runner passed me.

Then the pace car began to edge past me with it's lights flashing, and the first woman, Claire Kroshus was right beside me and slowly began to pull away. To this day I wish I had made more of an effort to stay with her.

Over the coming years, I would never, ever again have the opportunity that presented itself that day.

Claire was the last one to pass me and she would set a course record for women of 2:45:49 that still stands today.

I held it together as best I could because I knew it was still going to be a good result and when I crossed under the finish clock it read 2:54 flat.

It was a personal best by over two minutes, but I had lost 9 minutes to Claire in about 4 kilometers. Even if I had stayed with her for just two kilometers and then let her go, I would have broken 2:50.

Ultimately it was burning myself out at the very beginning of the race that was my undoing. Had I realized how much my overall endurance had improved, I may have been more cautious but it came as a total surprise.

If nothing else that marathon did bode well for the upcoming Ironman in August.

Unfortunately, with one week to go before Ironman Canada 1990 I took my bike out for one last spin. I had just had it tuned up and wanted to make sure everything was okay. It turns out the chain was not tightened properly and flew off when I was standing up on the pedals on an incline and I crashed and broke my collar-bone and that was the end of Ironman 1990.

At that point in my career nothing surprised me anymore. Besides, I had come to believe that the months and months of training and feeling so incredibly fit all the time in many ways was just as important as the race itself. So I did the only thing I could and what my nature dictated. I started training the next day for Ironman Canada 1991.

I couldn't swim or bike outside because I couldn't raise my arm, but my feet were not broken so the next day I was on the wind-trainer and back out running.

I felt a bit off balance because our arms naturally work in rhythm and synchronization with our legs and I had to keep the arm on the broken collar-bone side immobile against my body.

Even so, for a few weeks I could feel the ends of the broken bone rubbing against each other. One day I was running and the rubbing just stopped and I guess it was at that exact moment that the collar-bone set.

5

I was determined to make 1991 my big year for the Ironman. I told myself that this was the year that I could have the race I felt I was truly capable of.

Unfortunately I always made the mistake of buying into new training ideas in the hopes that it would make me more successful. That might be okay, but in 1991 I did it just 8 weeks before the race. That is not really the time to be making changes to a training program but every single year it seemed that I was yet another mistake and being taught a new lesson.

Another triathlete who was actually a swim coach told be about Hell week. He said it's what national class swimmers often did before a big event. They would have one week where they do monster mileage in the pool.

He suggested that if I do the same thing for the Ironman that it could make for a great result. What he suggested was a Hell week swim, a Hell week bike, and then a Hell week run, one after the other in the July before the upcoming Ironman Canada in August.

"Sounds good" I said, and that was pretty well the end of the conversation. I decided I would do the Hell week thing.

The idea was to push myself for six days and then take a rest day and the following week do the same thing with the next discipline. So the first week I swam 5k a day for 6 days. After each swim I went for a run of about 5-10 miles. Then I rested on the Sunday.

I had to take a week's vacation time in order to do the bike Hell week. For six days in a row I got up at 4:30am and got my bike ready, drove out to the highway, parked my car and rode to a small town 50 miles away and then came back. So it was exactly 100 miles. It took me around 6 hours. I did that for six days in a row then I took a rest day and started the run Hell week.

I ran 110 miles in 6 days and my Hell weeks were over. Actually, I

Ray Fauteux

didn't know it yet, but so were my hopes for my best Ironman ever.

When the dust settled on race day the clock said 12:27 almost exactly the same time as my two previous finishes. I felt tired all day out on the Ironman course and no doubt had used up much of my energy reserve somewhere out on those "Hell" weeks of training.

So I did the only thing I could do and signed up for 1992. I was going to do this until I was satisfied. I still felt that I hadn't taken quite arrived and hadn't taken the Ironman as far as I could.

6

When you train as hard as you can and seem to be treading water, perhaps it's time to look beyond the training and look elsewhere for a competitive edge.

Even today when they should know better, many athletes still do not fully understand the importance of diet when it comes to peak performance. At least when I began my career as an endurance athlete I had a bit of an excuse. There wasn't really much information about athletes and diet out there, at least not by today's standards.

I took it to heart when the luger told me about Dr Robert. Haas and his Eat To Win Diet. Dr. Haas claimed that by following his diet someone who was middle-aged could actually end up having the blood that you might expect to find in a teenager.

In other words you could be in your late 30's or 40's or even older and with the energized blood the equivalent of someone far younger, continue to perform at a high level at an age that is considered far past your prime as far as stamina, strength, endurance, and speed.

One of the great success stories of the Eat To Win diet was Martina Navratilova who shocked the tennis world by consistently beating the best professional tennis players in the world who were half her age. She would simply outlast them and they couldn't match her stamina.

One year after winning the French Open Martina was at the wrap-up dinner with Dr. Haas. When she looked at all the sauces and rich food the French are famous for the turned to Dr. Haas and said "help."

He looked over the vast buffet table and picked up two whole wheat buns and put them on her plate, because that's all there really was that stayed true to the diet.

Ray Fauteux

Dr. Haas claimed that far too many athletes would train themselves into the ground and then come up short when it counted because they didn't understand the importance of diet and how it could influence their performance.

I also learned that it was the same diet synchronized swimmers Michelle Cameron, Caroline Waldo, and Karen Larsen were on as they made their push for the gold medal in Seoul, Korea. I got to know their coach fairly well the year before the Olympics because every morning I would train in a pool adjacent to the Aqua-belles and would often talk with Pam the coach.

She swore by the Dr. Haas diet and you have to think that considering the level at which her athletes were performing, diet was taken quite seriously.

The diet must have worked for them because they won the gold medal.

I was looking for an edge during the training season that would perhaps help me perform better at the upcoming Ironman Canada triathlon in 1992.

I began to experiment with the diet in 1990 when I first heard about it but it was in the second year that I truly stayed committed to the Eat To Win diet. It was a diet that dictated high carbohydrate intake, some quality protein, and a minimum of fat. I pretty much lived on brown rice, pasta, potatoes, oatmeal, cottage cheese, skim milk, and whole wheat bread as I prepared for yet another Ironman.

The diet involves more, but essentially it was necessary to stick to the right combination of foods and supplements religiously over a long period of time in order to ultimately change the composition of the blood. If you cheat on this diet, the chances of it working for you are greatly minimized and the only one you are cheating is yourself.

I would not even bother trying this diet if you are not ready to commit to it for at least a full year. It takes at least that long to change the chemistry of your blood to a level that promotes levels of energy and endurance unlike you have ever experienced.

I even made my own bread and pasta sauce from scratch just to ensure that I knew exactly what I was putting into my body.

I happened onto a second competitive edge one day while on a training ride out in the foothills outside of the city. I ran into a hard-core cyclist and we talked as we rode together for a while and he told me about this electrolyte replacement drink that many of the long distance bike racers swore by, especially when they were in "century" (100 mile) bike races. It was called "Cytomax" and at the time was not available in Canada, but I was able to mail order it from the U.S.

In my quest to find the key to take me to the next level in the Ironman I was willing to experiment with anything legal that sounded promising and in the months leading up to the race I experimented with Cytomax and adopted it as my replacement drink for the upcoming race.

You can purchase Cytomax in Canada now but it won't do you much good. Like many perfectly legal and safe supplements that truly work and can be purchased over the counter in the U.S., when Cytomax was introduced into Canada the composition was altered and basically butchered to meet Canadian standards. Usually when this happens you will end up with a far less effective version of the original product.

For the year leading up to Ironman Canada 1992 I also adopted a different training philosophy. Instead of planning rest days ahead of time, I just took rest days when I felt I needed them. In hindsight that makes perfect sense. If you follow a set program religiously you will eventually end up training on days when your body demands rest or perhaps resting when you feel great and would really benefit from training.

Sometimes I would train 12 days in a row if I felt really good and then rest when I felt myself wearing down. On the other hand, it I rested and than trained for two days and still felt tired, I would rest some more. In other words, I no longer trained tired and I believe

Ray Fauteux

this is critical when it comes to preventing injuries and promoting the gradual growth of strength and endurance.

I also decided to do far less distance training(no more Hell weeks)and instead increased the intensity of the training sessions. For example, many experienced distance runners claim they can get just as much out of a 90 minute tempo run(fast pace just below race pace)as they would get out of a four hour LSD run(no, not the drug—Long, Slow, Distance).

Don't get me wrong, the long slow run still has it's place, but I did far fewer of them over the course of my training.

It was also this same year that someone suggested I look into chiropractic adjustments because often I would have neck, upper back, and shoulder pain from the repetitiveness of lane swimming and hundreds of miles draped over the profile bars on my bike.

So I found a chiropractor who worked specifically with athletes. He had pictures of some of his patients on his office walls and they included professional dancers, hockey players, football players, and world class bob-sledder's to name a few.

I was skeptical at first, but after 3 or 4 adjustments the aches and pains I had grown accustomed to all but disappeared. For the rest of the training year I would see the chiropractor twice a week.

So basically, those were four major changes I made to my training in order to try and break through the 12-hour Ironman barrier.

Ironman Canada finally arrived and while waiting for the starting gun in Penticton on Sunday, August 30, 1992, I had no idea what to expect and like every other race I had ever entered in my career, my intent was to do the best I could on the day and let the chips fall where they may.

7

I should have known in the swim that there was something unusual going on. My swim was a personal best time of 1:22:19 was a full six minutes faster than the previous year, the year of the Hell weeks of training. It was also about 36 minutes faster than my Hawaii swim in 1984.

At best I was a mid-pack swimmer and in the big scheme of things this was a pretty average time, but I remember thinking that I sure seemed to get to the turn markers fast. In hindsight I think what really happened is that it seemed really effortless because I was far fitter and better prepared than previous years.

If you go into an Ironman over-trained and tired as I did most years, then every part of the race becomes more of a struggle. Most years the swim seemed to go on forever and in hindsight it's most likely because I never truly understood how important rest was not just in the final taper weeks, but over the entire course of the training season.

I believe that as a result of that swim I felt really strong early on the bike and even the long climb up to the top of Richter's Pass did not seem as daunting as it had in previous years. The first real sign I had on the bike course that this was no ordinary year was when I hit the flat section at the back of the Pass.

Usually this was where I would begin to hit the wall in Ironman Canada and from there the rest of the day just got more and more difficult. I remember how amazed I was when I looked down at my bike computer and saw that I was zipping along at around 37km per hour. This is not super fast but for me it was a departure from barely being able to maintain a pace that was more like 25km per hour in other years.

I actually started to catch other cyclists as we made our way up the Yellow Lake hill. That's something else that had seldom happened in previous years.

Ray Fauteux

In the final charge down Main Street back in town I had to maneuver around other slower cyclists when normally I was really struggling at this point in the bike and it was other people passing me.

My bike time seemed like it was a lot faster than previous years, but by this point in the race I really wasn't aware of the splits and would see all this later on in the results book. The only time result I actually knew on race-day was for the swim because race announcer Steve King was calling out the times as the swimmers left the water.

After that it was all a blur and I was just intent on maintaining the best pace I could through-out the day. I never was one to fixate on each passing minute during an Ironman. By this time I had done enough Ironman races to realize that it's a long day out there and it doesn't take much for the wheels to come off. A solid swim and a great bike do not necessarily equate to a successful Ironman.

The best pro triathletes in the world can get swallowed up by the Ironman marathon if they have not paced themselves properly in the first two disciplines of the race. Year after year it happens to hundreds of age-group triathletes in every single Ironman, regardless what country the race happens to be in.

When the volunteers caught my bike in the transition and I climbed off, it was a really different sensation from previous years. Normally the stiffness in my back and legs was so bad it was difficult to even walk to the change tent. This year I took about two steps and I couldn't believe it. I had never felt this good and there was almost no stiffness.

After a 90 second transition, I ran up Main Street and out of town and by the time I started to make my way around Skaha Lake I was holding a pace that seemed comfortable and fairly easy all things considered.

I remember thinking about how fast I seemed to reach the ten mile mark.

As the marathon wore on I started to realize that I was running pretty damn fast for an Ironman race and became intent on holding the pace for as long as I could.

It was quite a treat for me to be out on the course when the leaders were coming toward me on their way back to Penticton. Normally I would be biking into town for the transition into the run and the leaders would already be finished the race.

It was pretty special to see the Puntos twins again as they were also competing in Penticton in 1992. The last time I had seen them was at the awards ceremony in Kona in 1984. As usual Sylvianne and Patricia were running side by side as we crossed paths out on the marathon course.

I reached the marathon turn-around just past OK Falls and was still holding what I began to think might be a suicidal pace and it crossed my mind that any minute a big hand was going to come out of the sky and squash me like a prairie grass-hopper on a pick-up truck windshield.

It was about here that I started to pass dozens and dozens of people. Power bars, water bottles, clothes, a lucky rabbit's foot, and just about anything else you can imagine littered the road.

People were hitting the wall in a big way and many were unable to go on anymore. There was chaos all around but I ignored it all. I concentrated on pushing outside distractions out of my mind and held my pace mile after mile.

I just threw in the part about the lucky rabbit's foot to see if you were still following along and not just skimming.

Anyway......

Every once in a while I would pass someone who was walking and suddenly they would be right on my shoulder and would try and run with me. One guy lasted for 15 minutes before packing it in. Others tried for 30 seconds and I would hear....."shit!" Or "damn it!" as they couldn't stay with me and would start walking again.

Ray Fauteux

I just ignored them all and didn't let their presence bother me. They could cave in or stay with me all the way to the finish line for all I cared. I was on a mission and stayed focused on what I was doing. I ran right down the center line of the aid stations and took one glass of water at every station and never slowed down.

I can tell you exactly what was going on with those guys who tried to stay with me after I passed them, because I had been in the same spot many times myself.

When you are in an endurance race like a marathon or an Ironman and are beginning to struggle and someone passes you it often seems like they are doing it effortlessly. Your first instinct is to latch on to them and try and run that same pace yourself. At first it seems like it should be easy to do because they don't seem to be running that fast as they pass you.

It will happen in your local marathon, in any Ironman race, and even in the Olympic Games. Even with the best runners in the world, if you are caught and passed in a marathon late in the race, it's virtually impossible to pass that person back.

The athlete who has maintained the fastest sustainable pace will ultimately finish ahead of those who have misjudged their pace.

What I was doing to those guys during the 1992 Penticton Ironman marathon is "exactly" what happened when Claire Kroshus passed me in the Calgary marathon.

At the time it looked like she wasn't running all that much faster than me and it seemed to take her forever to pull away, but I simply could not respond. Her "easy" pace translated into being 9 minutes faster than me and when the dust settled she had set the new course record for women.

As the day wore on and I got further and further into the Ironman marathon I stubbornly held the pace. I didn't eat at all and water was all I would drink for the entire marathon. I had taken in plenty of water and my replacement drink Cytomax, plus had eaten sufficient complex carbohydrates during the bike and felt great.

It was a treat not to have to deal with the nausea of past races that usually resulted from eating and drinking everything in sight.

It's a common mistake for triathletes out on the Ironman marathon course to try a bit of everything in search of something to eat that will make them feel better. Here's a news flash for you. There isn't one. As impossible as it might seem, your marathon from Hell will get even worse once you start trashing your stomach with flat pop, chocolate chip cookies, power bars, grapes, chicken soup, and anything else that isn't tied down on the aid station table.

With little more than 4 miles left to the finish line, I felt I was on a very fine line between caving in to the pace and being able to maintain it to the finish.

There is a very short and very steep hill just at the end of Skaha Lake just as you enter Penticton and make the final push through town to Main Street and the finish line on Lakeshore Drive.

As I reached the foot of that hill I saw four guys all walking as a group and pushing themselves to get to the crest of the hill. I knew that at this point I simply could not afford to give in to the hill or it might be my undoing. I knew that all I had to do was walk just once and I might never get started again. I went up that hill as fast as I could and passed all four guys. When I glanced back less than a minute later, I could hardly see them behind me.

That's the difference between running and walking and how easily 4 miles in the Ironman marathon can end up taking an hour or more to complete.

I knew now that I would be able to keep running right to the finish and when I reached the downtown area at the top of Main Street I could hear announcer Steve King at the finish line. In those days the finish line was right at the bottom of Main Street and there wasn't an additional few kilometers left to go before you reached the finish as there is in today's course.

Up to that point, I had no idea what my total race time was, but just knew that it was going to be faster than any Ironman I had ever been in. It didn't really sink in at first when I looked up at the official time as I crossed the finish line.

It registered 10:46 and I had just completed an Ironman race around one hour and thirty minutes faster than I had ever raced before.

It would be the next day when I saw the official results book for the first time before I would truly be able to see how the race had unfolded.

The swim time of 1:22 was a personal best by a few minutes and the bike time of 5:50 was my fastest time ever by over 30 minutes. It was the marathon time that was the real shocker for me.

My time of 3:34 was my best Ironman marathon by almost an hour. I had managed to maintain an 8:11 minute per mile average pace and it was good enough for 73rd fastest marathon of the day including the pros.

I had come a long way since the torrid King K. highway in Kona in 1984 when my marathon time was 4:58.

Come to think of it, I had come a long way from my couch potato days back in 1976 when I was inspired to get off my ass and do something with my life.

Can you imagine.

One day you can hardly make it up the basement stairs without stopping to rest and are too ashamed and embarrassed to even run outside, and 14 years later find yourself at 40 years of age holding your own out on an Ironman marathon course with the best?

I feel truly blessed to have been given the opportunity to live that experience.

To put it in perspective, the Puntos twins who were basically two of my idols back in Kona had marathon times of 3:29:23 and 3:30:31 respectively and I was mere minutes off of their marathon pace that day in Penticton. Of course they were faster than me in the swim and bike portions

Although I never returned to Kona, that finish time qualified me for the Triathlon World Championships in Hawaii. In 1992 I was in the 40-44 age category and there were 219 entries in my age-group and I had the 4th fastest marathon time.

My pedestrian swim times and the difficulty I always seemed to have going faster on the Ironman bike leg as usual cost me dearly and basically kept me off the age-group podium.

Just to illustrate the importance of "pace" in an endurance race like the Ironman, I'll use the example of someone in my age-group who finished less than two minutes in front of me that day.

He had a sensational 53 minute swim, a great 5:23 bike time, but blew up in the run and his marathon time was close to five hours. As I mentioned earlier, a great swim and bike do not necessarily dictate how an Ironman race will unfold at the finish line. It's the pace you maintain through-out the entire day that does.

Look at it this way, if the two of us were to combine our best swim, bike, and run, it would have resulted in a sub-10 hour Ironman time.

So to me the solution to achieving the next level and close in on the ten-hour mark I would have to find a way to cut 45 minutes off my swim and bike time combined and at the same time, not slow down in the run.

I still felt that there was more to come and I had not yet taken the Ironman as far as I could. I believe the reason I felt this way was because of how quickly I recovered from the race.

How on earth was it possible to have such a great recovery from the best race of your life and feel like a piece of crap after races when your race is two hours slower?

I still had not grasped the concept that fueling and hydrating properly, proper rest and recovery time all year long, and pacing race day properly is what dictated recovery and not what the timing

Ray Fauteux

clock read at the end of the race.

Unfortunately it took me years to figure all this out.

I wouldn't take that line of thinking into my preparation for the next year's race and made a classic mistake. I fell into the same trap that many Ironman triathletes do when they experience success.

8

There's a saying, "if it's not broken, don't fix it."

In hindsight, that's exactly the mind-set I should have maintained the following year after having my best Ironman result ever. But oh no, I had to go out and find a better bike that would be lighter, faster, and Hell..... even had tapered brake pads to cut through the wind.

Right.

Surely if I bought myself a bike that was $3000 more expensive than my aluminum "Nishiki Altron" I would be able to cut 30 minutes or more off my Ironman bike time.

Of course that's not true.

A Ferrari Enzo has amazing lines that are configured to cut through the wind, and it's one mean, fast-looking vehicle, but if you pulled out the V12 engine and replaced it with the 4-banger from the old Pontiac Firefly I was driving at the time, a Volkswagen Beetle would kick the crap out of that Ferrari in a drag race.

If you are either a pro triathlete or a very accomplished age-group cyclist a super-light, aerodynamic bike might make sense, but I sure was no pro and really not all that accomplished in the world of cycling. I was simply an average cyclist and there was no bike in the world that was about to change that any time soon.

It would have made much more sense to work on fine-tuning the engine of that Nishiki(that would be me)because I already had a bike that fit me perfectly and I felt very comfortable with.

Without a doubt, changing bikes after having a great result was one of the worst decisions I made in my Ironman career. I never felt "as one" with my new bike and always seemed to be fighting it, but that was not the only critical mistake I made in preparation for Ironman Canada 1993.

Ray Fauteux

All through the Spring and Summer before the August race I pushed myself hard on the bike. At least once a week for ten weeks in a row I did the same killer 4-hour bike route that was almost all hills.

I joined a Master's swim club and all though a freezing Winter would walk 5 blocks to and from the pool three times a week. I absolutely dreaded those swim sessions.

They did all these backstroke, butterfly, and breast-stroke drills that made no sense to me, because it was the front crawl I wanted to improve. Then they would haul out those freaking kick-boards and I would do one length while everyone else did ten laps. Sometimes I would kick until I turned blue and would go backwards. But I was told it would make me a stronger swimmer, so who was I to argue.

To make matters worse, on the way home my ass would freeze to the car seat in the minus thirty temperatures and that didn't help matters either.

By the time I found myself at the start line of the 1993 Ironman I was completely at a loss as to what to expect. It didn't take long to see the hand-writing on the wall. I felt like I was swimming in cherry Jello and when I got out of the water and heard Steve King call out the swim times, I was 3 minutes SLOWER than the year before.

I was really choked. I might just as well stayed home watching TV instead of dragging my sorry ass down to that pool in sub-zero temperatures night after night during the coldest winter since the dawn of civilization.

I had trained so hard all year that I was basically exhausted and to make matters worse, my top-notch, ultra-expensive, state-of-the-art, super bike started to shake and vibrate half-way down the Yellow Lake hill. It turns out the frame had a flaw in it and it waited until I was doing 80km per hour before revealing itself. It meant I had to brake the rest of the way down the hill in order to avoid a serious accident.

My transition times were more like ten minutes compared to 90 seconds from the previous years, and the marathon was a struggle from start to finish.

When the dust settled, I was right back to the 12-plus hour times of past years. My excitement at having such a successful race in 1992 led to a fixation on bettering my time had made me throw caution to the wind and almost everything I did made things worse and not better.

9

For the next eight years I tried everything I could think of to regain the form that had been so successful for me, but nothing worked. It's as if once I deviated from what had worked so well, I was never able to find it again. Even when I tried to emulate exactly what I had done leading up to that race there was still something missing.

I would make four more attempts at Ironman Canada after the 1993 season. In my search for the magic bullet I tried some very off-the-wall training methods.

I was still searching for something and although I didn't know what it was, my compulsive nature kept me moving forward.

One year I wanted to test the limits of my endurance and see how far I could possibly run in a week and then try out this over-distance training in a marathon to see if running "mega-miles" would make a difference in my race time.

I eased into it at first. I ran 80 miles a week, than 90, than 100 and every week I continued to increase the weekly total by 10 miles over an 8-week period. I used a 9:30 mile as an average time. I was usually running at a faster pace, but didn't want to inflate the figures so erred on the side of caution. So if I went for a 5-hour run I would divide 300 minutes by 9:30 to come up with the mileage for that run.

However, quite often I could check my time over a measured mile on one of my longer runs and I would be running around a 9:10 pace, so I know the total mileage figures are accurate and if anything, on the low side.

As I reached past the 120 mile per week mark I had to run twice a day. If I had a day off from work I would sometimes run 90 minutes in the morning and four hours in the evening. In about the 8th week I maxed out at about 160 miles. In order to achieve that, I had to run about 26 hours during that week. Once I started running over 120 miles a week I had to run seven days a week for several weeks on end in order to get in the distance.

I didn't bike or swim during this experiment.

I decided to enter the Las Vegas Marathon to see if the over-distance training would make a difference. Well, it did for about three quarters of the race, but I discovered that all that long slow distance training doesn't necessarily make you able to run faster. I took it out fast on purpose hoping that I would avoid the "wall" because of my mega mile training.

No such luck. I passed the 10k mark in about 37 minutes and was on pace for about a 2:43 marathon with about 8 miles to go and crashed and burned and ended up with a 3:03 finishing time. It was still pretty good, but not really worth the hundreds of miles of training I had run to get there.

What I discovered from that little experiment was that if you are going to train at an exclusively "long slow distance" pace, then don't expect your body to simply adjust to running faster than a speeding bullet if you have not trained for it. I would've had a far better result by running say, 60 miles a week and incorporating some faster paced tempo running into my training.

Ultimately I ended up with a severe case of plantar fasciitis and was forced to drop out of Ironman Canada the following August just 5 miles into the run.

Another year I tried Dave Scott's training program from the book he introduced in Kona at the 1986 Ironman. I followed it religiously for one full year and it was incredibly difficult. It was based on the majority of the training being done in interval sessions.

For much of the time I was training 7 days a week and would do all three disciplines every day. It was mostly speed work with some endurance training mixed in, but not that much. I would do intervals on my wind-trainer, do the same on the run, and then head over to the pool and do another 2500 meters of interval training.

One day I wanted to see how many running repeats I could do and did 50 repeats of 90 seconds at about 80% of my maximum with 30-second rest intervals in between. I ran slow during the rest intervals, but didn't stop. so ultimately I did a 100 minutes of running that morning and 75% of it was at about my 10k race pace.

It's not necessary to do that many repeats. I just did it to see how far I could push myself. It was just another product of my compulsive nature.

I think Dave Scott must have originally designed his program for pro triathletes, because it pretty much ended my career as I trained myself into exhaustion that year. It wasn't just the training, but the fact that I had a demanding physical job to maintain at the same time.

For some reason I never factored work into the equation and I can see where it would be far easier to manage an intense training program like Dave's if triathlon was one's only profession.

That year was the final time I was to enter Ironman Canada and four days before the race I developed severe insomnia and was unable to sleep more than a few hours in total leading up to the race. I did the swim and the bike and was taken off the course in an ambulance at about the one mile mark of the marathon.

To this day I still suffer from sleeping problems.

I believe deep-down that I knew I was given the opportunity to have the race of my life in 1992 and it would never happen again. I had reached the limits of my capabilities as far how "fast" I would ever be able to finish an Ironman race. Despite feeling that way, I still looked for answers and still pressured myself to somehow improve, and finally admitted to myself that it wasn't going to happen.

As the years passed, I was okay with that. The entire Ironman Hawaii 1984 experience would always be the most amazing time of my life and Ironman Canada 1992 would be the pinnacle of my amateur athletic career. I will always be eternally grateful for what both experiences have meant to me and how they have changed my life for the better.

However it left me at loose ends and I entered a stage in my career when I wasn't sure if I was a runner or a triathlete, so I guess I was a little bit of both.

Running was always special to me and for several years I competed in the 10k race circuit and did some marathons, but my Ironman days were not quite over yet.

10

It seems very strange to me that it was near the end of my Ironman career that I was introduced to the Total Immersion swimming technique. I mean, where the Hell was it all those years when I needed it? I suppose it was there, and I just wasn't fortunate to hear about it in those years I struggled so much in the swim.

Anyway, someone told me I should give it a try for my next Ironman. I was in my 50's now and had gone full circle when it came to the Ironman. I really enjoyed just being part of the event and no longer worried about how fast I finished the course.

I was no longer the same athlete after the years of intense training I had put my body through and I knew my Ironman days were numbered. I wasn't sleeping well and lacked energy so I always welcomed ways to make the day go easier out on the Ironman course.

As soon as I tried the total immersion technique I knew it would be the only way I would ever swim. I worked on the technique and came up with a swim strategy to keep myself out of trouble in the Ironman swim, and took it to the inaugural Coeur d'Alene Ironman in 2003.

It was the best Ironman swim I had ever had and I had never felt so totally relaxed. For the first time I went under 1:22 and swam a 1:17:22 that day. The best part of the whole thing was that I didn't have to swim thousands of laps to improve. It was more a matter of gaining an understanding of the natural buoyancy we all have and developing a long, smooth, and relaxed front crawl.

It turned out that Couer d'alene was having an incredible heat wave and it was 110 degrees out on the course that day. The race would eventually have the biggest drop-out rate in Ironman history up to that point.

Oddly enough, at that time Ironman 1984 and the inaugural Couer d'alene in 1993 were the two hottest Ironman races in the history of the event. I had the dubious distinction of entering and finishing both of them.

I finished the race just under 14 hours and if it had not been for that relaxed swim, I might've dropped out as well. I saved a lot of energy in the swim that I would really need later on.

There are three things that stand out in my mind from that inaugural Couer d'Alene race. One was the best Ironman swim I had ever had, two was the incredible heat, and the third thing was the gorgeous 20 something girl I ran with for several miles who all of a sudden just threw up on the side of the road.

She looked at me and said "do you know that until right now I have never thrown up in front of a man in my entire life"?

"Well" I answered, "I know I'll never be quite the same after witnessing it."

Anyway, she laughed and just kept right on running. Whatever happens out on the Ironman course always try and keep your sense of humor no matter how your day is going.

Just to be able to be part of the event is a gift and some races will be better than others, but just being out there is pretty special.

11

I really enjoyed being part of the very first Couer d'alene Ironman and decided to go back in 2004.

I really wasn't training all that much at this point and I think I realized that this would be my last Ironman. It was getting too hard to train as I struggled with low energy levels. I had become very aware that I had pushed myself so hard that I created underlying physical problems that wouldn't be going away any day soon.

It was also becoming harder and harder to enjoy the bike training out on the highway because of the growth of Calgary and the traffic on the roads and highways in and around the city. All in all I think I was just burnt out.

So I decided I would try something different and did all my bike training on my wind-trainer in my living room. I only went out on the highway about 3 times before the Ironman just to get used to being out on the road again. I had a two movie work-out that I did about once a month. I would tape two movies and when they were over, the training ride was done.

I ran a few days a week but really didn't do too much in the way of long distance. I didn't worry about the swim at all now that I had it figured out. It was just a matter of working on an economical stroke and all I really needed was about two swim workouts a week.

It changes your training mentality considerably if you really are not concerned about your Ironman time and just want to enjoy the experience.

The day was really going well. The swim was stress-free and it was really a treat to actually look forward to the Ironman swim after years of dreading it and feeling so out of my element. I guess the best way to put it is that from the very beginning of my Ironman career I looked at the swim as a necessary evil that I had to endure if I wanted to be an Ironman.

Everything was going great on the bike course up until I had just about finished the first of two 56-mile loops. As a matter of fact I was amazed at how good I felt on the bike despite having virtually no highway miles on the bike all season.

A few miles before the end of the first loop the roof fell in. I wasn't paying attention and my bike slipped onto the shoulder of the road. It was a sharp shoulder and it was about an inch lower than the road. My first instinct was to steer back up onto the road and that was a big mistake.

At 30km per hour my bike just went out from under me and I crashed onto my arm and shoulder. I knew right away that I had done some fairly serious damage, but hoped that perhaps it was just a bad bruise. I basically had to finish the entire second loop with just one arm because I couldn't put any pressure on one side. It made the fast sweeping down-hills a bit tricky, but I eventually made it to the bike/run transition.

The doctor in the medical tent said that I most likely damaged the AC in my shoulder. I wasn't really exactly sure what that was, but I couldn't raise my arm much past my waist. It was a lot like the time I broke my collar-bone.

For a few seconds I thought about calling it a day, but in my heart I think I knew that this could well be my last Ironman ever.

The Ironman had been far too good to me and done so much for me that in some way I felt it would be disrespectful to this great event to finish my career with a "did not finish" in the results book. I somehow felt that it deserved my best effort on that day regardless of the circumstances.

My bike time that day was 7:38:56 and my marathon time was 4:58:53. Oddly enough my finish time was 14:14 and was only 2 minutes faster than my very first Ironman in Kona in 1984.

So indeed, I had gone full circle.

A part of me hoped to be able to return to the Ironman when I

Ray Fauteux

turned 60, but it just never happened. I have never been able to find the physical energy level to attempt another Ironman.

However, this was by no means the last role the Ironman would play in my life, and in many ways it was the inability to train that would take my passion for the Ironman in an entirely new direction and for that, I will be forever grateful.

PAYING IT FORWARD

I decided to continue on running in 10k races because I really enjoyed them, and I thought perhaps it would be easier to find the energy to train enough to at least be competitive in my age group. The problem was that in all the years that I ran in races, beginning with that very first marathon, I always ran as hard as I could on race day. By that I mean I always tried to run the best time I could. To me that was what I enjoyed most about running and being in races.

Only three times over the years did I ever enter a marathon or 10k race and not give it my best effort. All three times I was pacing someone else to help them achieve a personal best.

Most of the time when I ran in 10k races I would end up in a sprint with someone in the final few hundred meters. Sometimes I would wonder if my heart would just explode in the middle of one of those all out sprints. It always amazed me how much the human body could be pushed. I'm not saying it's a good thing to do that, I'm just saying that it was in my nature to run that way.

When I decided to just stick with running for a while I was in my mid-fifties and for a few races was able to run in the 38:30 range for the 10k distance and it was pretty competitive time in that age-group, but then one day something happened.

I entered a 10k race that I had done many times in previous years and usually I could manage a time of around 38 to 39 minutes. It's safe to assume that as you age your speed will drop off by a minute or so every year, assuming of course that you were at basically the same fitness level. But on this day I simply did not have the energy to keep up the pace required to run the times I was accustomed to.

I crossed the finish line in 44:30 and was over 5 minutes slower than the previous year for the same course. That's a huge amount of time for a race as short as 10k. That was the first real big indication that something was not quite right and my "all out"

Ray Fauteux

racing days were coming to an end.

I decided I would take time off from any type of training or racing in order to see if the rest would be the answer to my overall lack of energy. It would be the first time in almost 25 years that I would go even a few weeks without training.

I had big hopes that one day I would be able to attempt another Ironman. I thought it would be pretty special to try and make it to Kona when I turned 60 and cross that same finish line 25 years after my very first Ironman in 1984.

It would have made for a pretty interesting set of finish-line images.

However it was not to be and even after consulting with half a dozen doctors over the years, there really seemed to be no definitive answer as to why my get up and go just got up and went. There were no answers to my insomnia, dizziness, lack of energy, and many other symptoms that I lived with on a daily basis.

Finally I found the answer at Group 23 in Calgary. They had doctors that specialized in treating athletes and they tested me for everything under the sun. All the myriad of tests came back negative and it led them to one conclusion. I was the victim of Over-training Syndrome. I had crossed the red line in training for so long that my body finally said no more. There is no cure for it.

Even now I find it very difficult to run three times a week for 30 minutes just to stay in shape or for the sake of fitness. It seems I needed a race out there somewhere in the future that I could focus on and I could train every day of the week as I visualized that distant finish line.

After making the decision to stop training I was left with a lot of time on my hands. My passion for the Ironman never diminished in the least just because I wasn't in the middle of the action. What I really needed was a way to take that passion and put it to good use.

2

I thought back to all that happened to me since that Summer day in 1976 when something I witnessed inspired me to change the course of my life. It struck me that it takes so little to inspire others and motivate them.

How many others were out there in the world in the same situation that I had found myself in years ago? How many people were out there living lives of discontent that were going nowhere? How many people just needed a small push–someone to believe in them perhaps–in order to get their lives headed in a new direction that would give them the opportunity to realize their true potential on many levels?

I thought of all that I had learned over the years. I thought of all the things I had done right and wrong and that just maybe if I could somehow pass on all that I had learned to others, it might just inspire them to live their own dream. At the same time it would let my passion for the Ironman live on even though it might not be on the race course.

It seemed to me that the best way to reach out to people was through the magic of the internet. If only I could build a website that people might want to visit. However, at 55 years old the world of technology had left me behind and I didn't even know how to get a computer going let alone build a website. I had used the computer at the library a few times but really had no idea what I was doing.

But I told myself that if I could get off the couch and run a marathon, and then learn to swim and become an Ironman, then sure as Hell I could figure out how to use a computer.

So on Boxing Day of 2004 I bought myself a $499 Dell computer and began another journey of self-discovery.

I'll never forget the day I brought my computer home. All those big boxes were pretty intimidating. A box for the monitor, a box for the

Ray Fauteux

computer, a box for the printer, and another one for the keypad. Oh yeah, and then there was a box full of electrical cords of all shapes and sizes. And I almost forgot about the 25 pounds of manuals and "easy-to-use" instructions.

Well, it took almost an entire weekend of deciphering those easy to use instructions before I finally got that sucker put together. Then some cable guy came over and gave my computer life and when he left there I was with an empty blue screen just waiting to be written on.

Just like a newborn baby that starts life with a blank blackboard just waiting to be filled with the lessons of life, I sat there with the whole world at my finger-tips. Now I just had to figure out how I was going to reach that world.

I played with that computer for days trying to find out how to build a website and with no computer skills I was pretty much lost. Finally I happened on to a site that said they could help me build a website even if I had little or no computer skills. So I took a leap of faith and sent them the $300 they charged for this service.

And so it began.

I struggled to build the site at first, but I persisted and did my best to follow the instructions that I was given. Finally I had the frame-work of my site built and then I struggled to build the first page to put on my new site.

I would spend a few hours writing something and then push the wrong key and my words would be sucked into a big black hole never to be seen again. It was truly the most frustrating few months of my life and many times I felt like giving up, but thanks to the confidence that I had built up because of running and the Ironman, I knew that if I persisted I would one day succeed.

Finally I figured out how to build a page into my new "rudimentary" website and began to type. I began to type out all the things that I had learned over the years. Soon I had three pages, then five pages, and then a dozen pages of information on my new website.

The yearly cost of my website included daily, weekly, and monthly stats about visitors to my site and where they came from. After I built five or six pages I would have three or four visitors a week and I just kept adding more and more pages. Soon I was getting 50 visitors a week and then 25 visitors a day. The more people responded to my writing, the more I wanted to write.

I did this for several weeks and still didn't have a name for my website. I just couldn't figure out the perfect word. To my way of thinking, it had to be short, meaningful, and unique. What I really wanted was a word that would describe the feeling I had in that very first moment when something inspired me to change my life. Like the day I decided that I wanted to run a marathon, and the day I just knew I had to do an Ironman.

One night in bed when I was just about asleep it hit me.........

IRONSTRUCK!

Right away I knew it was perfect. It had a hint of the Ironman in it, but also the image of a bolt of lightning that gets your attention and spurs you to action. It didn't hurt that it was also a very compact, easy name to remember. It was perfect.

I'm sure I was holding my breath when I Googled Ironstruck, because I was well aware of copyright issues and knew I could not use the word if someone else owned it. I couldn't believe it. It would be the first and only time I would Google something that would come up with this result.........

"No hits on the world wide web."

It seems that the two words had never been put together in any context until that very night. So that's how Ironstruck got it's name. I liked it so much that I copyrighted it and now own the rights to Ironstruck.

Almost six years have passed since I bought my $499 computer home and I just want you to know that I am writing this book on that same computer. Really, I believe the sky is the limit and real success will happen the day I finally figure out how to reach all the people in the world who could benefit from Ironstruck.

Ironstruck has become an extension of my Ironman career and although I may not be in the water with 2700 others doing a 2.4 mile swim, or climbing a hill into a headwind on some Ironman course somewhere, I feel that I am out there right beside all those who have been inspired and motivated by Ironstruck to take on the Ironman challenge for themselves.

I truly believe what has contributed most to Ironstruck's success is the fact that I have never forgotten what it was like to confront the Ironman for the very first time. Because of that I can write in a way that people can understand and appreciate.

As one fan of Ironstruck said after reaching her first Ironman finish line in Lake Placid, "It's like you were right there with me. Everything you said would happen, did happen".

3

For almost two years I worked on trying to make my website a place where people would enjoy coming to visit. From the very beginning I wanted Ironstruck to be a welcoming place, especially for those who were new to triathlon or perhaps had a dream of becoming an Ironman.

I made it a mandate from the very beginning that anyone from anywhere in the world could email me with their questions, thoughts, doubts, or concerns and I would help them as much as I could from my own experience and to the best of my ability.

I made it very clear from the beginning that I was "not" a pro triathlete or certified coach and never pretended otherwise. I wanted them to know that I was just an ordinary person who had the chance to live his dream and wanted to help them live theirs. I made sure my visitors understood that what I share with them is what I learned from my years out on the Ironman and marathon highway and they could take it or leave it.

The email questions began coming from all over the world. There was no question that I ever considered dumb or unworthy of an answer. Triathlon and the Ironman in general is taking the world by storm and many times I would hear from people who really knew nothing about triathlon, but often after witnessing an Ironman for the first time, just couldn't get it off their mind.

For lack of a better word, they were "Ironstruck". After every single Ironman event in the world there are spectators who witness ordinary people achieving something extraordinary and they are so moved by what they see they become just as Ironstruck as I was when I saw my first Ironman on T.V. in 1982.

The power of the strange, almost hypnotic attraction the Ironman exudes is something that almost defies logic, but it is as strong a force now as it was a quarter of a century ago. What I find especially intriguing is that it seems to pick and choose those who have the most to gain by answering the challenge.

One day in 2006 I received an email from twin brothers from South Africa who were very definitely captivated by the Ironman. It always amazes me how inspiration can come from the strangest places. The email they sent me once again altered the direction of my life.

You just never know when opportunity will knock on your life's door and you have to be ready for it. It might be a gentle tapping or an insistent, unrelenting pounding, but for God's sake, get up and answer the door!

I learned early on in my amateur career that there is a risk with opening the door to a new adventure, but it's the risk of failure that makes success so special.

The brothers who emailed me were just a week away from their first Ironman and were entered in Ironman South Africa in Mandella Bay.

They said they loved my Ironstruck website and were using the information on it as their guide for the big race. "We are copying all these pages from your website to take to the race with us as reminders" they said. Then he typed the magic words.

"Why don't you write a book?"

Well, I had never considered writing a book. To me that was something other more accomplished, gifted, articulate people did, not some guy with barely a grade 12 education who seldom paid attention in English class.

But it you have read this far, you know what happened next.

If I could learn to run and become a marathoner, learn to swim and become an Ironman, and learn you how to use a computer and build a successful website, then why couldn't I write a book and become an author!

Why not indeed.

I became just as determined and compulsive with my writing as I was with my running from the moment I laced up those grass-stained runners some 30 years earlier. In less than four months I self-published "Ironstruck...The ironman Triathlon Journey." In the process I gained a new respect for all the first-time authors in the world.

Writing a book is a remarkably scary thing to do. I mean, I had "no" idea what it would be like to put my thoughts into the pages of a book and wonder if anyone will even like what you have to say. For an introvert like me it was a huge step, but by this time I had figured out that there is an element of risk in striving for anything in life that's worthwhile.

So like it or not, Ironstruck the book was born and I'm so glad I took the suggestion of the brothers from South Africa who inspired me to once more step out of the box and take a chance.

That first book proved to be just the beginning of my writing adventures. In 2008 I realized from all the questions I was getting from novice Ironmen from all over the world that there was a need for a Triathlon/Ironman Question and Answer book. So I sat down and wrote out 500 questions and then answered them from my own experiences.

They were questions I would have loved to have had answers to in those early days when I began my Ironman career. Of course nobody had any answers back then because triathlon in general was still in it's infancy in the early 1980's.

The best thing about writing these books is that I get to go to triathlon and marathon expos all over the country and meet amazing people and talk triathlon and running with them.

It was during these book signing sessions that I met many health care workers and teachers who were very concerned with the lack of fitness in the youth of today. Obesity had become epidemic across North America and kids who were not yet teens were being

Ray Fauteux

diagnosed with type-2 diabetes.

So I felt there was a need to write a book for teens and pre-teens that might give them some insight into fitness, a healthy diet, and basically how to maintain more balance in their lives.

"Lifestruck...a better way for today's youth" would be the title of my third book and through it I hoped to inspire kids to include some regular fitness and a sound diet into their lives.

So what if you can't make the school team? I suggested they give triathlon a try because they didn't have to please anyone and could have fun, learn new skills like swimming for instance, meet some new friends, and more importantly, stay fit.

It's very surprising to me just how many adults, like myself for instance, did not learn how to swim early on in life. You would think with about one-third of the world covered in water that it would have more importance just from a safety point of view.

So if being part of something like the Kids Of Steel program gives youth the opportunity to be confident in the water, that in itself is a huge accomplishment and will benefit them all their lives.

My fourth book was inspired by the people who would stop by my table and say, "well, we can't all do the Ironman. Why don't you write a book for beginners"?

What a great idea and it was these people who inspired "Triathlete In Transition" a book for the beginner triathlete and along with Ironstruck Q+A and Lifestruck, it would be my third book in 14 months. I was on a roll and much like my running and Ironman career I knew that if it was in my heart, that one day I would succeed as a writer.

As I'm writing this page in book five for you I can't help but wonder at all that has transpired since I took a chance and ran those first few gasping laps around a gym over four decades ago.

It is almost too difficult to contemplate that had I not taken those first few steps I would have missed out on so much. How do I put a value on so many unforgettable memories of special people, places and distant finish lines that at one time seemed so far beyond my grasp?

More importantly, I have been able to pass on to others all that I have learned over the years and just possibly inspire them to experience the thrill of accomplishing goals that at one time seemed so far out of their reach.

4

One of the main reasons for writing this book that you are reading right now resulted from a re-occurring theme I have encountered at marathon expo book signing's.

The majority of people who have Ironman on their mind make the transition from an endurance running background as opposed to a swimming or road-bike background.

So much like myself, they might swim like a rock and the last time they were on a bike was when they were 11 years old, but it doesn't seem to matter. That is of course, if they are truly "Ironstruck".

I'll give you an example of what I mean by that, and this happens all the time.

A marathoner will come up to my table to talk and will say something like, "I'd really like to do the Ironman but I know I never will because I can't swim".......or "don't like swimming"........or "I'm afraid of the water".

That has nothing to do with it.

It's like saying, "I'd love to drive a car across the country, but don't know how to drive".

What?

So why not learn how to drive and get a license if that trip is something you would truly love to do. Why would you want to spend so much time "wishing" you could do something and not ever doing it? Is it because it takes a little effort or perhaps requires you to take a risk?

Well obviously if you are a marathoner it's neither of these reasons because you have what it takes to go as far as you already have.

To my way of thinking, the real reason is that it's not all that important to you to become an Ironman or else you would find a way.

When someone tells me they can't swim and as a result won't ever be able to experience an Ironman, what they are actually telling me is that it's not really in their heart to become an Ironman in the first place. Let's face it, if it was a passion they would look past any obstacles in their way and be focused on reaching that finish line no matter what it took.

I don't ever try and pressure anyone into taking on the Ironman challenge even though they might have all the physical tools to become an Ironman. Their possibility of succeeding at something as daunting as the Ironman is greatly diminished if becoming an Ironman is not close to their heart.

That's why it's also vitally important to take on the Ironman challenge because it's something you truly want to do and not in order to please someone else. Your biggest weapon as a novice Ironman is your passion to reach the finish line and without that passion to draw on when the going gets tough in training and the day of the race, you will be at a serious disadvantage.

Sometimes out on the Ironman bike course the day grows into something far different from an athletic event and having the necessary emotional and mental strengths to push through mile after mile when your body is begging you to stop become key components of your ultimate success.

After talking to hundreds and hundreds of people about this very subject, I have gotten very good at reading them and discovering pretty quickly if a person is truly Ironstruck and believe me, it would simply blow you away to meet some of the people who are.

Some of them look as far from an athlete as you could ever imagine. They might be tall, short, young, old, over-weight, and the list goes on and on.

But none of that matters.

Ray Fauteux

I can see it in their eyes when they say something like, "I want to be an Ironman"....or "I want to cross that finish line"....or "I don't care what it takes, I'm going to do it".

These people all have something in common. They have been totally captivated by the Ironman and want it so bad, they don't have time to worry about bothersome things like learning how to swim, getting on a road bike for the very first time, or perhaps losing 80 pounds. They just go and do it.

They are just as Ironstruck as I was the day I just knew I was going to answer the call of the Iron Gods and cross that finish line any way I could.

There is also no doubt in my mind that one day they will realize their dream.

All I'm saying is, don't tell me you can't be an Ironman because you can't swim, or think the down hills on the bike might be too fast, or because you can't afford it, or.....or.....or.

You can respond like some people do and just say, "it's not something I feel I really want to do", or "it's something I have on my bucket list for one day down the road", or "I'm happy just being a runner".

All of those reasons make perfect sense and you are very definitely preaching to the choir if all that is truly stopping you is learning how to swim or ride a road bike.

If you have read this far than you know that at one time I was about as far from an Ironman as you could possibly imagine and the entire premise of this book is that if you want something bad enough it's not as impossible as you might think.

IRON TIPS

As I mentioned earlier in this book, whenever I can I like to pass on any thoughts and suggestions I have that might just prove helpful for someone who is new to triathlon or possibly preparing for their first Ironman.

I go into much more detail in my previous three triathlon books about many topics that will be instrumental in helping people realize their Ironman dream, but still I think it's important to include my thoughts on some of the more important elements of the Ironman in this book as well.

These are areas where I made some of my biggest mistakes in my Ironman career and therefore, make me somewhat of an expert on "what not to do".

Perhaps you are a marathoner who is determined to become an Ironman and I convinced you to buy this book. Or maybe you are a competitive swimmer or accomplished cyclist who doesn't run all that much.

Maybe you have already done a few Ironman races or perhaps you have done a lot of them.

It doesn't really matter. I still feel I should take the time to pass on some of the more important points I have learned over the years concerning the Ironman.

I don't presume to know everything about the Ironman and what I write in any of my books comes from my own experience and misadventures and as always, you can take what you find helpful and leave the rest.

Regardless of where you happen to be on the Ironman stage, perhaps I can pass on a few things about this great event that might help you achieve your best Ironman result, regardless if it is your first or 21st attempt.

Ray Fauteux

NEVER STOP LEARNING

Even today, years after crossing the Ironman finish line for the first time, I am learning something new about this amazing event all the time. The Ironman is constantly evolving and even though I may no longer compete, I continue to try and learn all I can through interacting with other triathletes and researching relevant information sources so I can pass on what I have learned to others through my books or during face-to-face conversation.

I truly believe that one of the best ways to succeed and excel at just about anything is to learn from others who have lived the experience and are willing to pass on what they know to you.

Despite my best intentions there are some very accomplished Ironmen who I occasionally come across at an expo somewhere who see my banner that says "EVER THINK OF BECOMING AN IRONMAN" and they swagger on over with the thought already embedded in their head that there is nothing they could ever learn from me or one of my books.

It boggles the mind that some people think they have nothing to learn from others. Especially when it comes to the complexity of an event like the Ironman that has so many variables.

How do they know they have not been doing the same thing wrong over and over again for two dozen Ironman races? I really believe we can all learn from others on a continuous basis no matter how superior we are in ability or how much faster we can reach the finish line in the Ironman or for that matter, life in general.

I can usually tell an Ironman cut from this mold just by the way they walk towards me with the "I'm an Ironman, I'm really going to show this guy" look in their eye or by the way they pick up one of my books without really looking at it as if saying, "there's nothing I can learn here, just wait until he finds out I'm already an Ironman."

So when I say to them, "So, how many Ironmen have you done?" it usually catches them by surprise because they didn't have a chance to tell me yet that they have done any.

Meeting all sorts of people in my travels is what I enjoy most about attending triathlon and running expos through-out the race season.

What I have noticed most is the ability I have gained to be able to read people after just seeing their mannerisms or perhaps just talking to them for a few minutes.

I can't help but feel especially connected to people who are taking on the Ironman for the very first time. I think it's because the memory of my first Ironman success and what it meant to me is as vivid as it was the day it took place so long ago.

I'm sure my passion for the Ironman has become quite obvious to you by now and regardless of where you are in your own personal Ironman Triathlon journey perhaps I can shed some light on a few things that might possibly be helpful in making your experience just a little more enjoyable and successful.

REST IS YOUR FRIEND

Probably the main lesson I learned over all the years of running and triathlon is that our body, even though it might be a miracle of creation, has a limit to the amount of physical stress we can bombard it with. I believe that one of the main keys to enjoying Ironman success is incorporating enough rest into the equation on a regular basis during the months of training leading up to the race.

Sure you can survive an Ironman by running, swimming and biking every day of the week in preparation for the big day. Yes, of course you can go out on a 50-mile bike ride in the mid-day heat three days before your Ironman, but in reality you will often be leaving your best race-day effort out on the training course somewhere and will go into your race over-trained and tired.

I often think that one of the reasons I managed to finish my first Ironman in Kona in 1984 was because of my lack of knowledge about the event, I never killed myself training. I was mainly concerned to just learn how to swim and I had my running endurance to fall back on.

Ray Fauteux

I did no hill training or wind-sprints or intervals and if anything was grossly under-trained as far as the bike. But at least I was not going in tired like I did in many Ironman races later on in my career when I mistakenly believed that more was better.

The wind and the heat of the 1984 Hawaii Ironman caused quite a few people to drop out. If I had gone in over-trained and tired I most likely would not have survived the conditions of that particular race.

Yes of course you want to make sure you prepare yourself much better than I did that year, but at the same time always giving your body time to recover from the rigors of training and racing simply cannot be stressed enough.

Believe me, it is very easy to get excited when you realize success in your triathlon and running endeavors and the natural reaction is to enter race after race in order to live the experience over and over. Soon you find yourself looking for marathons and Ironman races all over the place and always have some sort of stress happening to your body.

It's another misconception that you can enter a marathon or an Ironman just for the fun of it and take it easy and consider that giving your body a rest, but it's just asking for serious injury problems if your idea of rest is to do a major endurance race at an easy pace.

A marathon is a marathon and an Ironman is still an Ironman and you are still stressing your knees, muscles, and joints for 26.2 miles or for the entire Ironman course no matter how slow you go.

The problem is that in your exuberance you are risking injury that just might be shortening your career. I know that's exactly what I did and now I am dealing with the consequences.

I was so looking forward to competing when I was sixty, sixty-five, and even older. I really believed that these would be the years that I would be the most successful racing against my peers in my age-group and perhaps earn the right to return to Kona one more time.

However I was my own worst enemy and at 55 years old my competitive career pretty much came to an end because I pushed myself to the limit for so many years. I began to think I was invincible.

Total rest really means "no" swimming, biking, and running for an extended period of time.

When you see so many amazing athletes 60 years old and older just imagine how long "your" career can be if you are a thirty-something or forty-something and you play your cards right? By Ironman standards you are still a Spring chicken and could easily have a career that lasts another quarter of a century.

If you have an endurance career that's a way of life and has been ongoing for years, what would it hurt you to take a full year off from all competition and serious training every three years or so and give your body a break?

You don't have to lose your conditioning completely in your recovery year, but relaxing swims and easy, short early morning runs will be enough to carry you over until you feel ready to begin training again in the future.

It's not at all surprising that some athletes have their best performances ever after giving their bodies an extended break. It's not unlike world class swimmers who are forced to quit training for long periods due to injury or illness. The forced rest often does wonders and shortly after they return to action they often have personal best results.

Besides, I think taking an extended rest is a great way to get back into touch with the other important aspects of your life like family and friends who have sat patiently by and supported your athletic career.

WE ALL HAVE DIFFERENT ABILITY

If you are a runner and are just beginning your Ironman journey than there are several things to consider. Everyone is at a different stage of athletic development so no two people will ever prepare the same for their first Ironman.

For instance, there is a huge difference between knowing how to swim and just having to build swim endurance, as opposed to having to learn how to swim from the very beginning.

If you are an accomplished runner or better yet, a marathoner who knows how to swim I really believe you could sign up for an Ironman that is perhaps one year away and be successful in reaching the finish line.

However, if you have to learn how to swim from the very beginning and perhaps have never been on a road bike, then I think you could do very well by giving it two years as it takes a while to become a competent and confident swimmer and proficient at handling a road bike.

MORE IS NOT ALWAYS BETTER

It's a misconception that you will lose your endurance if you don't keep running a long distance at least once a week and don't hammer out 100 mile bike rides whenever you can. If you are swimming, biking, and running on a regular basis than it's safe to say that you can cut back on the extreme distances and pick the proper time to incorporate distance into your training.

Normally you will have the most success by building up your distance and endurance slowly over time and adding some longer distance training sessions in the last quarter of your training year. A few longer rides at that point in your training will get you used to being on the bike for an extended period of time like you will be on race-day.

It's much more important to work on proper technique in the early months of your training and focus on "how" you bike, swim, and run, and not "how far and how fast".

For instance when it comes to bike training, it would be far wiser to spend time working on a proper "spin" technique than it would be to hammer out 100 mile rides with poor body positioning and poor technique that can lead to needless injury because you are not incorporating the big muscle groups in your legs to your best advantage.

Dave Scott said once that if you can do half the required distance of the Ironman run and bike in training and still feel strong, than you will most likely be fine on race day. It's not necessary, and often not the best strategy, to bike a hundred miles or do 25 mile runs week after week.

As I said earlier in this book, I tried biking monster mileage with no success and I tried running monster mileage with no success. You simply don't need it and would be far better off doing half the amount and resting more.

Rides of half the Ironman distance done at a good steady pace will ultimately have you in good enough shape to survive any Ironman bike course in the world.

It's really a great advantage to be able to train in three different disciplines and it's the main reason why triathletes in general do not get injured as often as those who are just runners.

You will be doing the ultimate in "cross-training" and as a result stressing different muscle groups at different times.

If your arms and shoulders begin to hurt from all that work in the pool, then cut back on swimming for a few weeks and bike or run a bit more. If you feel a twinge in your knee when you run, than take some time off from running and swim more.

It's all about balancing stress and rest and understanding that less is not more and that there is a time and place to add distance to your training. Technique, technique, technique should be your mantra as you begin your Ironman journey.

Ray Fauteux

THE IDEAL IRONMAN SWIM

Once you are confident you can do two miles in the pool without requiring an oxygen tank when you climb out, than it really serves no great purpose to do that distance over and over. You would be far better served to work on becoming a smoother, more efficient swimmer.

What's the point of swimming 4000 meters three times a week if you have a poorly developed swim stroke? All that means is that you are reinforcing bad habits into your muscle memory.

You would be far better off to swim 1500 meters of structured drills that break down your stroke while teaching you proper buoyancy and the best way to achieve an energy-saving, relaxed front crawl swim stroke that will ultimately make you a far better swimmer.

This will do you far more good on Ironman day than trying to be a faster swimmer. There is simply no benefit to be had by knocking yourself out in your months of training in order to shave five minutes off your Ironman swim. Overextending yourself in the Ironman swim could ultimately add two hours to your marathon time.

Visit "Total Immersion". Terry Laughlin has the best swim technique for triathletes all figured out with his Total Immersion swimming concept. It pretty much changed the way I approached the Ironman swim and for the first time I began to truly enjoy the Ironman swim and not fear it.

Sadly, Terry passed away, but he left quite a legacy for the triathletes of the world. The last time I looked, others have carried on with the Total Immersion website.

Beginning your Ironman with a swim strategy that keeps you out of traffic problems and a swim stroke that is effortless and smooth is without a doubt one of the biggest keys to your success on Ironman day and will help you realize you goal of reaching the finish line.

UNDERSTANDING NUTRITION

When I really got into running I had myself convinced that I could eat as much as I wanted and never gain weight.

Actually, that was true. I was running so many miles that it never mattered how big my bowls of butterscotch ripple ice cream were. I basically leveled out at 150 lbs. and stayed there for pretty much my entire athletic career regardless of what I ate.

However, it's not really calories and weight gain that should be the biggest concern when it comes to how you are fueling your body through all those weeks and months of training.

Your food choices are vitally important because what you eat and drink during the course of the training season will ultimately dictate the quality of fuel that powers your body. In turn, that fuel dictates your energy and endurance levels and nothing could possibly be more important if you are preparing for an Ironman.

It's not really rocket science.

Maintain a healthy balance of complex carbohydrates, proteins, and quality fat. When in doubt of what a good balance should be, you might want to consider the 40-30-30 Sears diet. It's a good starting point, but it's essential that you make wise food choices just the same.

The best carbohydrates are complex as opposed to simple. For example, whole wheat bread, brown rice, potatoes and yams, pasta, and salads were the mainstays of my diet all through my endurance career. I stayed away from simple carbohydrates like cake, cookies, ice cream, soft drinks, and donuts just to name a few.

My favorite fats were olive oil and coconut oil. Most of the remaining fat you will require will be naturally occurring in the quality carbohydrates and protein you eat.

For protein I preferred egg whites, skim milk, yogurt, cottage cheese, and a quality protein powder.

Ray Fauteux

You might want to get your hands on a book called the "Eat To Win" by Dr. Robert Haas that I mentioned earlier. It was written over 40 years ago and I still believe it is the best nutrition advice I have ever come across for building energy and endurance through the power of diet.

There is no way to tell anyone what they should eat and drink during an actual Ironman race because everyone is different.

The smartest thing you can do is experiment with replacement drinks and different varieties of food in the course of your training until you find what works best and than use that food and drink combination in your Ironman.

GEARING UP

Today's novice Ironman is inundated with the variety and quality of Ironman bikes, wetsuits, and clothing on the market today. They are made to believe that the key to their success hinges on the net worth of their bike and the rest of their spiffy triathlon gear.

Nothing could be further from the truth.

Yes, it's great to be able to dress to the nines with the finest of triathlon clothing on the market and have a super-light $5000 bike. If money's not an issue than go crazy and treat yourself because you have earned it

And yes there are triathletes who are so advanced and skilled that the best of equipment will benefit them, but that's not the case for about 95% of us.

Don't think for a minute that because "you can't afford it" it's impossible for you to take part in an Ironman.

To me it's very disheartening when I run into people who you just know are totally "Ironstruck" but feel taking a run at an Ironman is simply out of their financial grasp.

I do all I can.

I give them a free copy of Ironstruck...The Ironman Triathlon Journey" and do my best to convince them that there are ways to get it done.

I really believe there is always a way to get there. So what if all you can afford is a $300 road bike you bought at a police auction?

So what if you can't afford a skin tight tri-suit? Dave Scott was winning Ironman Hawaii back in the early 1980's with his t-shirt flapping in the wind.

The total value of my gear for Ironman Hawaii 1984 was about $400. That includes the bike.

Can't afford the high cost of a motel at the Ironman venue? Go with three friends or family members and pay just 25% of the cost. Or take a tent and camp like I did for several Ironman races.

Hell, you can even rent wetsuits now if all you want is one shot at the Ironman.

Your ability to realize your Ironman dream is not predicated by the tapered brake pads on your bike, the millimeters of thickness in the rubber of your wetsuit, or orange-tinted $300 sunglasses.

It's what's in your heart, your desire, and your passion that will ultimately get you to the finish line and you should never give up on finding a way.

CREATIVE COMPULSIONS

I'm sure some of you are asking yourselves why anyone would train so hard that their body would finally rebel and just give out and bring their running and triathlon career to a crashing halt.

Well, when you have a compulsive personality like the one I'm sure I inherited from my misguided youth, it doesn't really matter if you are doing drugs, drinking, or running; you simply can't seem to stop.

I know with a certainty that I have met many, many people who approach their running and triathlon ambitions the same way I did. If you really think about it, you have most likely encountered your own share of runners or triathletes over the years who train and compete compulsively.

I'm sure there are many people out there who would never admit to being in the clutches of a disorder spawned from a dysfunctional childhood that would eventually have an impact on everything in their life.

In many ways I feel I owe my deceased alcoholic father a vote of thanks, because he has unknowingly dictated the course of my life through his alcoholic tendencies.

It was tempting for a while to give in to self pity and place blame on him for all that was wrong with my life.

There comes a point in our lives where we can accept "what was" and refuse to place blame. We have the option of taking control of our lives and using our compulsive personalities in a positive manner.

It was in my nature to set a distant goal and not give up until I did everything I could to reach it. It's how I was how I was able to do whatever it took to finish a marathon, learn how to swim and become an Ironman, learn how to use a computer and write 5 books in four years.

To put it more simply, instead of an alcohol or drug addiction, I became addicted to running, the Ironman, and writing. Ultimately I developed a passion for all three.

I would take that trade-off any time and do not regret a minute of the experiences it afforded me. So if you find yourself consumed by the same compulsive inclinations, embrace them and use them to your best advantage.

Creative compulsions can be a mighty force and can supply the necessary drive to make the seemingly impossible, possible.

The one word of warning I should give however, is that it's important to temper your compulsive creativity. If I had been able to harness my compulsive training and racing and allowed sufficient time for my body to rest and recover, I would still be active in running and triathlon.

However, I do believe that things happen for a reason, and had I continued to compete, Ironstruck would never have been born. There would be no Ironstruck books.

I believe in fate and that every single thing we do impacts not just our own destiny, but also the destiny of the people we touch in the course of our lives.

So I can't help but wonder about emails I have received over the past few years that are much like this one....

"I live in Swakopmund, Namibia. I'm 39 years old. Within a year I went from fat to fit enough to complete Ironman South Africa in 16:12:39 enjoying every minute of it. I gave up smoking and my whole outlook on life changed. Once you've done an Ironman, you can do anything!!

Reading your book Ironstruck changed my life forever. Thanks so much."

So am I sorry that I pushed myself so hard that I had to give up competing? How can I be when it ultimately resulted in the creation

Ray Fauteux

of Ironstruck and would one day have an impact on someone in need of inspiration on the other side of the world and change their lives for the better, forever?

Through this whole life experience of the past 45 years I have learned that we all have the ability to inspire others through our actions, and if there is one thing that is in short supply in the world, it's inspiration.

I believe that Ironstruck still has the potential to help many, many people around the world.

Once I was asked how I would describe what Ironstruck stood for in one short sentence.

I didn't have to think about it very long because it has basically been the story of my life.

"Become more than you ever thought possible."

END

*** This book was originally written in 2011. I came back to it in 2023 to update some information and also to fix typos etc. I also gave it a new cover. At 73-years-old I still continue to write, run(slow short distances), swim, and weight lift in order to stay fit.

I also continue to write. My two latest books are:

It's Kona Calling(An inspirational fiction book based on the Ironman Hawaii race I completed in 1984). This was my first fiction book.

Just the other day I published another fiction book called **The Nomad Club** about a teenage girl who started a club in her school to stop bullying. All my books are available on Amazon.

Writing is just like everything else in my life. Once I started, I can't seem to stop.

Thank you for reading this book. I hope you found it at least a little helpful and entertaining.

Ray

Printed in Great Britain
by Amazon

26709525R00096